S0-BNH-783

THE VILLAGES
OF NORTHERN FRANCE

Normandy's Pays d'Auge

THE VILLAGES
OF NORTHERN FRANCE

ANDREW SANGER

PHOTOGRAPHS BY JOHN MILLER

This book is dedicated, with thanks, to my parents Joe and Hilda Sanger
for giving me an early love of French life and language,
and to Gerry and Joshua for their companionship as we travelled together
on many journeys through rural France.

BY THE SAME AUTHOR

Exploring Rural France
Languedoc & Roussillon
South-West France

Front cover: The waterfront at Bergues
Back cover: A typical Alsatian house

First published in Great Britain in 1994 by PAVILION BOOKS LIMITED, 26 Upper Ground, London SE1 9PD

Text copyright © Andrew Sanger 1994   Photographs copyright © John Miller 1994

Designed by John Youé and Alan Grant

The moral right of the author has been asserted

All rights reserved. No part of this publication may be reproduced, stored in a retrieval system, or transmitted, in any form or by any means, electronic, mechanical, photocopying, recording or otherwise, without the prior permission of the copyright holder.

A CIP catalogue record for this book is available from the British Library

ISBN 1 85793 155 6

Printed and bound in Hong Kong by Mandarin Offset

2 4 6 8 10 9 7 5 3 1

This book may be ordered by post direct from the publisher. Please contact the Marketing Department.
But try your bookshop first.

Eurotunnel would like to point out that the views of the publisher and author of this book are not necessarily those of Eurotunnel.
Le Shuttle is a trademark of Eurotunnel.

CONTENTS

The author and publisher have tried to ensure
that all the information contained in this guide is as
up-to-date and accurate as possible; many of the
practical details such as addresses, telephone
numbers, closing days, etc., have been supplied by
the establishments themselves and are correct at
the time of writing (December 1993).
Although every care has been taken in the
preparation of this guide, no liability for any
consequences arising from the use of information
contained herein can be accepted by Eurotunnel,
the publisher, or the author.

General map

- Channel Tunnel terminal
- Motorway
- Major Road
- River
- National Boundary
- Département Boundary
- Major City/Town

A 2 - E 314
A 13 - E 313
Maastricht
A 4 - E 40
Cologne
3 - E 40
15 - E 42
Liège
Meuse
A 4 - E 411
A 26 - E 25
E 27
E 421
A 3 - E 35
A 48 - E 44
Rhein
Frankfurt
Mainz
Darmstadt
LUX.
GERMANY
N 43
LUXEMBOURG
A 6 - E 50
Mannheim
ES
MEUSE
N 18
Saarbrücken
A 4 - E 25
N 3
A 4 - E 25
Metz
MOSELLE
Karlsruhe
N 35
Meuse
A 31 - E 21
A 4 - E 25
N 4
MEURTHE
ET-MOSELLE
N 4
Nancy
N 4
STRASBOURG
N 67
Marne
N 57 - E 23
Meurthe
N 59
BAS
RHIN
N 83 - E 25
A 5 - E 35
Rhein
N 74
A 31 - E 21
Epinal
Colmar
A 35 - E 25
Freiburg
HAUTE-
RNE
N 19
Chaumont
VOSGES
N 83
A 5 - E 54
Langres
N 19 - E 54
Mulhouse
Saône
N 19 - E 54
Vesoul
Belfort
A 36 - E 54
HAUT
RHIN
Basel
N 3 - E 60
Dijon
A 31 - E 21
N 57 - E 23
A 36 - E 60
ZÜRICH
SWITZERLAND

INTRODUCTION

Until today, the British have been at a disadvantage. At long last, thanks to the Channel Tunnel, we too can enjoy a pleasure which other nations have long considered natural. We can set off for a few days (or even a few hours), whatever the sea conditions, at any time of year, without great preparations, without undertaking a sea voyage, simply to savour the delights of the countryside, culture, customs and cuisine of our next-door neighbour. Never again need our hearts sink as we approach the coast of Kent and notice an ominously rolling sea. Instead, drive on and drive off without even seeing the water. Rain or shine, Le Shuttle takes about thirty-five minutes, from platform to platform, to reach France.

A sea voyage it certainly used to be, across a great psychological and physical barrier that lay between Britain and the Continent. The Channel – even at its narrowest navigable point, 34 kilometres of often choppy water – had to be crossed, and even in modern ships with safety announcements about 'muster stations', check-in times and the captain's message about the state of the seas, a sense of adventure was

Vineyards of Alsace

generated. Now, a simple national border is all we have to cross.

It is liberating, too, not having to 'catch' anything. Le Shuttle passengers can pack at leisure and set off from home when they are ready, without haste or anxiety. Le Shuttle is correctly named: it is a shuttle service between Folkestone and Calais that runs throughout every day and night of the year, carrying passengers and their vehicles on specially designed shuttle trains. There's no need to worry about a departure time or reservations. Tickets are bought on arrival at the terminal, although they can also be purchased in advance (see page 11). At peak times there will be up to four departures an hour when fully operational.

Once on the M20 in Britain, you are already well on the way for a clear drive through to some of France's great cities of history, art and culture, as well as colourful street markets, fine shops and first-class French restaurants. Big names like Reims, Rouen, Nancy and Strasbourg and, of course, Paris should be visited at least once. For those who in the past have been daunted by the Channel, now is the time to see what you've been missing.

Yet while the towns and cities have so much to offer, there are riches to be discovered on a rural ride. Indeed, touring in the French countryside, travelling from village to village on uncrowded minor roads, is sheer delight. The country means more in

A Norman farmhouse

The Villages of Northern France

France than in Britain. It is full of living history, vibrant tradition and local pride. Old customs and festivals remain popular, regional dishes are served, local building styles are jealously conserved and (even where farming is on a large scale) local produce holds its own at the family dinner table.

Nearly every village has its qualified baker (*boulanger*) who makes fresh bread on the premises twice a day, and a pastry-cook (*pâtissier*) whose delicate pastries and cakes are likewise freshly prepared in his own kitchens. Unassuming villages and little towns often have a good, reliable restaurant offering hearty classic dishes and local specialities. Many provincial communities are able to boast a truly great restaurant, acclaimed in French food guides like the *Guide Gault Millau*: the whole region, town and county alike, will look to them for a leisurely celebration meal. Then, of course, rural towns and villages may also have other modest attractions, a *musée* or château, picturesque streets and charming scenery.

How much easier it is to enjoy these country pleasures than to grapple with the traffic and the parking in big towns! Having parked, strolling is quiet and unhurried in a little town or village. Driving from place to place presents no traffic problems either. Thanks to a high proportion of the population living in country areas, and a total population density only half that of the UK, France has the benefit of an excellent network of little-used but well-maintained country roads linked into an extensive, high-quality *autoroute* (motorway) system.

Le Shuttle travellers arrive in France just south of Calais, with direct *autoroute* access from the Tunnel. *Autoroute* A16 heads southward to Boulogne, western Picardy and beyond into Normandy, or northward into western Flanders and across the Belgian border. The A26 runs southeast towards eastern Flanders, the Ardennes, Champagne and beyond (on the A4) to Lorraine and Alsace. Turn at the junction of the A26 with the A1 (near Arras) for a quick run to eastern Picardy, to Paris and points south.

Or you can ignore these fast highways and leaving Le Shuttle's Calais terminal, meander on minor roads; for example, through the pretty, rolling back country of Artois and Picardy behind the Channel coast. Head down from here into Upper Normandy, down to the woods and castles and monasteries of the Seine Valley, and across the river to the delightful, apple and cream country of the rustic Pays d'Auge.

Obviously, there's no right order to visit the rural regions of northern France. But from Normandy you might skirt north of Paris to reach the beech forests and grand, Gothic spires of eastern Picardy. A small step across the border with Champagne brings you into quite a different land, of immaculate vineyards, high, airy fields, broad vistas and villages dedicated to making the world's most festive wine. This in turn leads

LE SHUTTLE'S TRANSPORT SERVICE

Eurotunnel's cross-Channel Le Shuttle services operate on a turn-up-and-go basis, regardless of sea conditions, twenty-four hours a day, every single day of the year, between terminals at Folkestone and Calais. Passenger vehicle shuttles carry cars, coaches and motorcycles in either single- or double-deck carriages, depending on the height of the vehicle. Separate freight shuttles carry lorries.

Once fully operational there will be up to four passenger vehicle shuttle departures per hour during peak periods. Even during the quietest periods of the night, there will always be a minimum of one departure per hour.

How to use Le Shuttle

1. Exit the M20 motorway at junction 11a straight into the Folkestone terminal. At the toll booth, purchase your ticket by cash, credit card or cheque. Tickets can also be bought in advance from selected travel agents or from the Le Shuttle Customer Service Centre at Cheriton Parc, Folkestone, telephone (0303) 271100.
2. After passing the toll booth, you can visit the Passenger Terminal where you will find duty-free and bureau de change facilities as well as restaurants and shops. Alternatively, you can head directly for Le Shuttle.
3. Pass through British and French frontier controls. Both frontier controls are situated at the departure terminal only. On the other side of the Channel, you drive directly off Le Shuttle and straight on to the motorway without further frontier controls.
4. Head for the allocation area where you wait to drive on to Le Shuttle. Attendants will direct you down the loading ramp and on board. Drive through the carriages until an attendant directs you to stop.
5. Turn the engine off and put the handbrake on. Loading takes about eight minutes and then Le Shuttle departs. During the short, 35-minute journey, you remain with your car inside the spacious, well-lit, air-conditioned carriage. Stay in your car and relax, perhaps tune into Le Shuttle radio. However, you can get out of your car to stretch your legs.
6. On arrival at Calais, attendants will direct you to drive to the front of Le Shuttle and out on to the exit ramp. This leads straight to the exit road and on to the motorway network. There are no further controls and, just over sixty minutes after leaving the motorway in Kent, you are heading off into France. Remember to drive on the right!
7. On the way home, leave the A16 *autoroute* at junction 13 which leads directly to the Calais terminal. From here, you repeat the process described above.

naturally into, and across, the green hills of the Vosges to reach the wine country of Alsace, perhaps the most exquisitely charming of all regions. You could return through Flanders, which has a secret: it's not all coal mines and factories. This northern borderland, too, has pretty areas and villages of charm.

Nor is there a correct order to visit a region's villages. However, for convenience, in each chapter of this guide a route has been proposed leading naturally from one village to the next. Sometimes a good country hotel or restaurant has been recommended along the way, but for fuller information on where to stay, where to eat and what to bring back home, look at Le Shuttle's other guides, *Small Hotels and Restaurants in Northern France and Belgium* and *Shopping for Food and Drink in Northern France and Belgium*.

Access to the little towns and villages of northern France has never been so convenient. Indeed, 'convenient' does not properly describe the improvement on everything that has gone before. Le Shuttle gives the freedom to get in the car and simply drive across the border to that good life, fine food and quiet *joie de vivre* of rural France. The Continent won't ever seem the same again.

Driving in France

On leaving the Calais terminal, two important rules of the road need to be remembered: first, drive on the right, and second, give way to traffic from the right except where signs indicate to the contrary.

If you are not used to driving on the right, bear it especially in mind when merging, joining a motorway, overtaking, or turning a corner – all of which may tempt you into the left lane.

The second point confuses some people, but is simple enough. The rule is *priorité à droite* – give way to traffic from your right – except where signs show that you have priority. The usual sign, which does not exist in the UK, is a yellow diamond: it means that your road has the right of way. If you

see a yellow diamond crossed out, that's a clear warning that you may have to give way to traffic coming from your right. And of course, Stop signs and Give Way signs (which look the same as in the UK) show that you must give way.

Priority can be important in town centres and also on country lanes, where sometimes there are no signs. However, you never have to give way to vehicles coming on to the public highway from a private drive or farm track.

Roundabouts can be a problem, especially for the French, who are still not used to them. It is certainly not true that *priorité à droite* has been abolished at roundabouts (as stated in some guides and information leaflets) and care should be taken, especially in town centres and in rural locations with little traffic.

A wine maker's sign in Champagne

LE SHUTTLE HOLIDAYS

Le Shuttle Holidays, Eurotunnel's tour-operating division, offers an attractive range of breaks, combining pre-booked accommodation with a return trip on Le Shuttle. For further information, and to obtain a copy of Le Shuttle Holidays' Breaks brochure, visit your local travel agent or telephone (0303) 271717.

A Give Way sign on the approach to most roundabouts has the words *Vous n'avez pas la priorité*. This shows that, just as in Britain, you must give way to traffic already in the roundabout. If there is no Give Way sign, people in the roundabout must give way to you – and likewise, once in the roundabout, you must give way to anyone joining it.

One other point to remember: on-the-spot fines. If you break any driving regulation, the police may take the details and fine you. For example, for failing to come to a complete stop at a Stop sign, they can ask for (at the time of writing) 900 F. If you cannot pay, they may keep the car as security. They do not take credit cards, but Eurocheques are acceptable.

Formalities

Technically, a passport is not required by citizens of EU countries travelling within Europe, but both France and Britain have retained the right to demand identification papers bearing all the information carried by a passport.

For driving, an ordinary British driving licence and insurance papers are recognized in France (you should have them with you). In the event of an insurance claim, you may need to have been issued with a Green Card by your insurance company, failing which they may limit your cover to Third Party, Fire and Theft.

The Tunnel Story

Eurotunnel's construction of the Channel Tunnel marked the realization of a dream first discussed over two centuries ago. Excavations were actually commenced in the 1880s at Shakespeare Cliff, near Folkestone, and at Sangatte, near Calais, but abandoned. Then in 1986, Eurotunnel won the concession from the British and French governments to design, finance and operate the Channel Tunnel. The time was at last right to build a tunnel linking Britain with France. The decision was made at government level that it should be a rail tunnel.

Work again started from Shakespeare Cliff and Sangatte. For sheer technical accomplishment, the completion of the Channel Tunnel was one of the greatest engineering achievements of all time. Not one, but three 50-kilometre-long tunnels were dug through solid rock between

25 and 45 metres beneath the sea bed, two for the rail services and one for maintenance access.

The three tunnels allow the operation of shuttle services carrying freight vehicles and passenger vehicles between Folkestone and Calais by Eurotunnel's Le Shuttle, and through-train services on the Eurostar service, which is run jointly by the railways of Britain, France and Belgium.

The Eurostar trains, which are based on state-of-the-art French rail technology, can run on all three rail networks, initially at speeds of up to 300 kilometres per hour, allowing a journey time of about three hours from London to Paris and three hours ten minutes to Brussels. For more information about rail services through the Tunnel, call the Eurostar Information Line (0233) 361 7575.

Just across the Channel, inland from Calais, all around the Channel Tunnel terminal, or down the rolling, clifftop coast towards Boulogne, a pleasant countryside combines farms and forests, large-scale agriculture and small-scale rural life. Scenic, wooded valleys cut across the region. Despite a sprinkle of manufacturing around the edges of large towns, this remains a profoundly rustic part of France. Wherever the land is high and open, nearly flat arable fields expand to immense size. Where the countryside is hillier, farms contract to a miniature, old-fashioned scale.

There's wilderness and wildlife here, too, and a sense of the grandeur of nature, especially the vastness of the sky. Along the coast south of Calais, the Côte d'Opale, majestic cliffs (giving clear views across to the coast of Kent) separate huge, sandy beaches. Further south, the immense river estuaries of the Canche and the Somme have created a windy, reedy world of marsh and sand called the Marquenterre. Home to a multitude of sea birds and waders, this has been designated a wildlife preserve. Inland, much of the area falls under the protection of the Parc Régional du Boulonnais, a pretty, hilly area of small farms and beech forests. The Channel Tunnel terminal lies on its border.

However, Man has also made his mark on this peaceful landscape, and in the worst way. Those fields of vegetables and grain once were battlefields. Not just in this century, but through the ages, this has been the ground on which many battles have been won and lost, much blood spilt. Generations of British soldiers have fought here, sometimes against the French (as in the Hundred Years War), sometimes with the French (as in the First World War).

Historically, this area was not Picardy, but Artois – a forgotten region, a borderland which at the French Revolution became the Pas de Calais département. (The old province of Picardy became the Somme, Oise and Aisne départements to the south and east.) Artois stood on France's frontier with Flanders, and there was much overlap of cultures, as there is still. A French town like Arras could have a strongly Flemish feel. Yet today French Flanders (the Nord département) plays the role of border country, while Artois has slipped into Picardy, already a huge territory which reaches from the Channel almost as far inland as Reims, the capital of Champagne 250 kilometres away.

In the Middle Ages, though, Artois was a distinct entity and, together with western Picardy, its ownership much disputed between rival monarchs. It lay exposed, always vulnerable to attack from either Flanders or from England. The Hundred Years War, that bitter struggle between England and France for the French crown, began in 1337 – and lasted rather more than a hundred years. Most of its landmark battles were fought here. The first major clash was at Crécy in 1337 when Edward III of England soundly beat the French forces. Despite occupying much of the area, the English were not able to consolidate their hold on the region. In 1415, under King Harry (Henry V) they again joined in a great battle with the French, at Agincourt. Again, the English won a decisive victory, but once more could not keep control of the conquered territory.

Gradually, in a succession of engagements, the English lost their foothold in Picardy and Artois. They managed, though, to cling on to Calais right into the sixteenth century. When she lost it to the French in 1558, Mary Stuart knew that an era had come to an end. She grieved: 'When I am dead and opened, you shall find "Calais" lying in my heart.'

Numerous neat, well-tended little Commonwealth War Cemeteries act as a reminder of more recent conflicts which brought destruction on a vast scale to this part of France. Battle sites of the Great War can be seen near Arras, at Vimy, and on the road from there to Amiens. Throughout the region, signs of the two world wars have not been completely erased, nor, perhaps, should they be. They have become almost part of the soul and character of the villages and small towns of western Picardy, a symbol of the enduring need to rebuild, to plant

Seafood is a speciality

again, to continue normal working life, to live in peace with one's neighbours.

Indeed, Man has not only destroyed here, but also built – and on a grand scale. From the thirteenth century to the eighteenth, prosperous Artois textile towns like Arras constructed fine squares, mansions and grandiose civic buildings which have survived (though largely rebuilt after war damage). Picardy also nurtured the Gothic style of architecture, and it flourished here. The flamboyant style, in particular, found expression in western Picardy. There can be no better example than at Amiens, capital of the Somme *département*.

A busy industrial town, Amiens lacks charm, but is dominated by its magnificent Notre Dame cathedral. The largest (in area) in France, and among the most beautiful, the building was protected from bomb damage during the Great War simply by being covered with sandbags. It stands on the site of a Romanesque cathedral destroyed by fire in 1218. Much of the present Gothic masterpiece, including the glorious west façade with its deep portals filled with sculpture, was complete and in use less than twenty years later, although construction continued for several hundred years more.

The pleasing towers, of unequal height, were added in the fourteenth and fifteenth centuries. Inside, the cathedral is of majestic, inspiring proportions, and has superb stonework and rose windows. There are memorials to the British and Commonwealth soldiers who died here in the First World War.

Two much smaller towns are far better known to the British: Calais and Boulogne. Of the two, Boulogne – just 25 kilometres by the A16 *autoroute* from the Channel Tunnel – has the greater appeal as a town to visit and explore. Its hilltop *ville haute* (upper town), enclosed within medieval ramparts with a walkway on top, preserves a quiet atmosphere, cobbled streets and many historic buildings, including an unusual, domed church visible from all over Boulogne. At the foot of the hill, the waterside *ville basse* has a lively air, a small, manageable shopping district with some excellent food specialists, and a colourful street market in Place Dalton. Fresh fish is sold on the quaysides. Among other attractions in the town, fish can be seen in a different light at Nausicaä, a giant state-of-the-art aquarium complex beside the sea in Boulevard Ste-Beuve.

By contrast, Calais – some 4 kilometres from the Tunnel – though very ancient, presents a more functional, modern appearance. North Calais, the 'old quarter', retains few vestiges of the past other than a curious medieval watchtower in Place d'Armes. This, though, is the district for hotels and restaurants. Across an encircling canal, south Calais is the larger, busier 'new quarter' with many shops covering the gamut of choice, price and quality. The two districts meet at the distinctive Calais landmark, a tall Flemish-style twentieth-century town hall belfry with a bright orange clock-face. At the foot of the belfry a sculpture by Rodin represents six burghers of Calais, leading citizens of the town who offered their lives if Edward III would spare the rest of the population. In the event, the conquering English king did not harm the citizens of Calais.

A century ago, or even half a century, the most distinguished town on the western Picardy coast was Le Touquet. A haunt of the well-to-do British, a lavish resort with casino and opulent hotels, the resort had a reputation for high life, glamour and style. Perhaps surprisingly, that has by no means vanished. Wealthy young Britons still frequent its smart hotels, some of which retain a good deal of untarnished Edwardian polish. Millionaire villas hide in leafy woods on the edge of town. Private planes still come and go at the small airport. The promenade enjoys fine, airy views across an open expanse of flat sand.

All three of these coastal towns offer good restaurants with high-quality local dishes. The cuisine of the Picardy coast favours simple, straightforward preparations, especially of fresh fish and seafood. Perfect *pommes frites* (chips) are the most typical accompaniment. You may also come across *ficelle picarde*, a traditional rolled pancake filled with ham, mushroom and creamy sauce. Spicy sausages and *pâtés* are popular too, and cheeseboards feature all the strong, pungent specialities of Picardy and Flanders (most of which can be bought, by the way, at the excellent cheese shop Olivier in Boulogne). A light beer is the northern drink, and many locals prefer it to wine with their food.

The village route through western Picardy travels from the Channel Tunnel, through the Bolonnais regional park, to the Somme estuary, coming within easy reach of the three main coastal towns and inland Amiens. On the way, it takes in Gothic churches and abbeys, historic battlefields, wild country and peaceful, pretty farmland.

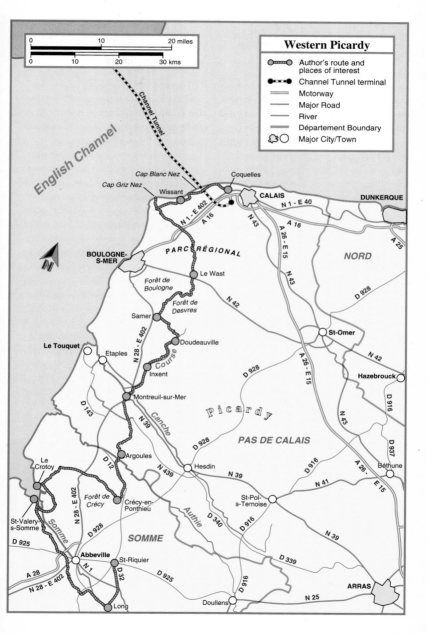

Western Picardy

COQUELLES
Beside Channel Tunnel terminal

First village in France for Le Shuttle travellers, Coquelles knew that life would never be the same again as soon as it was chosen as the site for the Channel Tunnel terminal, which is largely within the borders of the *commune*. It has embraced the changes with enthusiasm, seemingly delighted to have been put firmly on the map – and on the *autoroute* signs.

The main square is now Place de la Concorde (*concorde* implies international harmony). One bar, on the main road just off the square, has been renamed as Café du Transmanche, or the Cross-Channel Café, while the other, the old-fashioned Coquelles bar and restaurant, has reacted by putting out the flags of European nations. Signs have even been put up proclaiming Coquelles as part of a new Cité de l'Europe commercial development to be created around the Tunnel terminal.

For the moment, though, it remains a village, a typical small community of the north. Like many another in this region, it suffered during two world wars, and had to be quickly patched up, so can hardly be considered pretty – even locals would agree. Not all charm has been lost, though. Tractors, hauling trailers loaded with hay, park outside the bar. Simple, low, brick houses and a few modest shopfronts line the street. Some windows are brightened with flowers.

It's also a convenient place to stay, close to the Tunnel and *autoroute*, with a couple of modern budget hotels on its edges, and with none of the traffic or parking problems associated with looking for a room in Calais.

WISSANT
On D940, 16 km south of Calais

The road between Calais and Boulogne along the Opal Coast gives glorious views across the Channel to the gleaming chalk cliffs of Kent. Two great headlands rise high, Cap Gris Nez and Cap Blanc Nez, and on either it is a pleasure to stop and enjoy the sea, the air, the light and the panorama.

Between the two, the road descends into the village of Wissant. The place depends on the sea, draws its livelihood from the sea, and clings to the sea, yet is not beside the water. The name means 'white sand' in Flemish – and soft, pale sand there certainly is, a vast expanse of beach which separates this fishing village from the water's edge.

The fishermen of Wissant have devised a curious means of overcoming this obstacle. They *drive* their boats from seashore to village. The trawlers are loaded on to trailers and pulled by tractor into the streets of Wissant. There they park outside houses, or even in the village car park beside the church. Some fishermen drive their boats into the streets to sell their fresh catch straight from the deck.

Come out of season. Not just the fishing boats, but equally the broad sands with their views of the two Caps and the English coast, have made Wissant something of a tourist trap in high summer. Cheap eating places spring up on the sand, and coaches bring visitors. There's a breezy beach-side roadway, traffic free, where tourists stroll. On the flat seashore sail-karts sometimes hurtle by.

The old church, Wissant

Before and after the brief summer rush, Wissant remains quiet and hard working. The brick houses are low and simple, many being just a ground floor with dormers in the roof. The centre of the village is the triangular Place de Verdun, with an old stone church along one side, a *boulangerie* and hotel-restaurant on another, and on the third, the more imposing Hôtel Normandie, so-called for its painted-on, Normandy-style 'beams'!

LE WAST
On D127, 15 km east of Boulogne and 35 km from Calais

There comes a point, heading south and east away from the airy, flat fields of the coast, when the country changes abruptly. It becomes greener, hillier, more pastoral, much prettier. At that point is Le Wast.

Only a tiny village (the name is Viking and does not mean 'vast'!), it might be thought damned from the start by having quite a busy D road passing through the centre. But its considerable charm overcomes this. Neat lawns with carefully tended flower beds line the offending through-road. There's a small central square, perhaps better

Le Wast's village green

described as an open space, dominated by a handsome mature chestnut tree. It looks almost like a village green, not a common sight in France. Around it are some low cottages with steep roofs, a couple of decent restaurants and a hotel, and a more imposing house set back behind its gateway.

This dignified seventeenth-century mansion, the Manoir du Huisbois, can be visited and contains the information office for the Parc Naturel Régional du Boulonnais (the Boulogne Regional Nature Park). All of the lovely country surrounding the village lies within the boundaries of the Park, and the office has details of walks and drives, local events and places of interest nearby. Just drop in to learn more about this satisfying corner of Picardy.

Stroll the few paces up a short backstreet from the green to the church and it becomes plain that little Le Wast does possess one treasure, the superb carved portal of the Romanesque church. It used also to have a Renaissance château, which has become the Hôtel des Tourelles, just on the village boundary.

Manoir du Huisbois and Parc Naturel Régional du Boulonnais office open March–Oct., all day weekdays, p.m. at weekends

SAMER
Beside N1, 15 km south of Boulogne and 49 km from Calais

Although it stands beside the main *route nationale* to Paris, the small town of Samer has a pleasant, cheerful, villagey air. It consists of little more than its large, triangular, cobbled main square. Green hills of pasture are in view all around. Cafés, shops and bars, and the Hôtel du Croissant, stand on the sides of the *place*: most of the buildings date back to the eighteenth century.

At one end of the square, cafés crowd up to a dignified church doorway. The tables of the little Café de la Place stand on the cobblestones in front. These unseemly, newer buildings almost completely conceal the lower part of the church. The upper part, however, especially a fine hexagonal stone tower under its black conical spire, rises above the roofs to dominate the village centre.

Inside, the handsome Gothic church is powerfully

The cobbled main square at Samer

atmospheric, dimly lit, white-painted, rib-vaulted, with a brick ceiling. Once, this was part of a great Benedictine abbey, founded thirteen hundred years ago. The ancient abbey was destroyed by the Normans in the eleventh century – but rebuilt. It was to suffer again at the hands of successive invaders over the centuries: in 1346, 1412 and 1540 the abbey was destroyed and reconstructed. But at last it died, and today only the church remains. The public areas of the *mairie*, in the square, contain a few fragments of carved stonework from the abbey.

Its illustrious times long past, Samer lives on as a small market centre for a pretty and rural corner of Picardy. The town is especially known for its strawberries.

DOUDEAUVILLE
On D127, 23 km south east of Boulogne and 51 km from Calais

The Course is a mere trickling stream, hardly a river at all, running gaily through grass and meadows, with woods and green pasture rising on both sides. Yet its valley, winding through the quiet countryside southeast of Boulogne, is sheer delight. Not every village along its length is especially

*Doudeauville:
the château-ferme*

pretty, and in places there are rather too many new houses,
as people have been drawn by the valley's peace and
gentleness. It seems that everyone though, whether in a new
house or old cottage, feels that they must live up to the
beauty of their surroundings. Everything is freshly painted
and attractive, hedges clipped, and gardens thrive with
abundant flower beds and vegetable patches.

A few villages along the Course have been blessed with
exceptional charm. Doudeauville is full of gardens,
exquisitely placed on the last slope of a green hill. Below an
unassuming church, cluster the white-painted houses
adorned with flowers, and a seventeenth-century *château-
ferme*. And at the bottom, beside the little valley road, flows
the flooding Course, crossed by tiny, wooden bridges.
Above and behind the village, sheep graze calmly. Leafy
woods cover the crest.

INXENT
On D127, 15 km east of Boulogne and 35 km from Calais

Continuing down the country road which follows the green valley of the little River Course, it might almost be possible to pass this hamlet without noticing. In fact, it is one of the most delightful places on the route. A few simple, low houses, mostly white, mostly just a single storey, line the edges. In front of them and hanging at the windows, abundant geraniums splash colour. From the ground bursts greenery and huge hydrangeas, heavy with blooms.

The tiny, rustic *mairie* ('town hall' is too grand a translation), with white walls and pale blue door and window frames, might be a farmer's cottage but for the hand-painted sign and official-looking notices pinned to the door. On the wall one of the antique, dark blue plaque 'signposts' – useless for anyone travelling faster than walking pace – gives distances up and down the road, to the nearest hundred metres.

Behind the *mairie* stands the 200-year-old parish church with a new, black spire. A few yards further along, on the other side of the road, the most appealing building in the village satisfies the eye, the soul, and the stomach: the gorgeous little Auberge d'Inxent, with its white and blue shutters and overhanging greenery. The garden of the Auberge leads down to the bank of the Course. There, a narrow bridge of rickety, wooden planks crosses the water. On the other side, a lovely, shaded, waterside path runs among trees, grass and flowers.

The Course flows for a few miles more, closely followed by the country lane, to reach the wider valley of the River Canche. Across the Canche on its hill rises historic Montreuil.

MONTREUIL-SUR-MER
Just beside N1, 38 km south of Boulogne and 75 km from Calais

Hardly a village, but a busy little market town with a long past, Montreuil 'on sea' is now a full 15 kilometres from the coast. Hard to believe now, as you walk the footpath around the grass-covered brick ramparts looking across flat farmland, that in Roman times Montreuil was actually a port. The original hilltop village was destroyed in its entirety by Holy Roman Emperor Charles V in 1537, but rebuilt, and only in the last few years has spread on to lower ground outside the walls.

A cobbled roadway – which used to be the *route nationale* to Paris! – winds through the town from the fortified brick gateway on the north side through to the immense, triangular Place Général de Gaulle and the gateway on the south. On the way, it passes Place Darnetal, a much smaller square at the top of the hill. This square is charming with its cropped lime trees and small hotel, the Darnetal. Round the corner is the flamboyant Gothic chapel of the *hôtel-Dieu* (infirmary), which, in its small interior has lovely glasswork and fine carved wooden panelling. Facing it across the square, the rather patched-looking walls of the war-wounded St Saulve church, much repaired in its 900 years of history, still makes an impressive sight. Originally, this was the Romanesque church of an abbey which stood here, but thanks to repairs and

A backstreet in Montreuil

rebuilding carried out in the twelfth and thirteenth centuries, it became a fine piece of Gothic workmanship. The deep porch, elaborately carved, is especially striking.

Some of the side streets, too, have kept their cobbles and old houses, and deserve a leisurely stroll. Close to Place Darnetal rise the gaunt walls of Montreuil's extensive Citadel, a second fortress within the town ramparts. Great towers and an empty moat guard the imposing gateway. Inside, it's rambling and unkempt, with curious fragments of ruins and strange subterranean chambers where the coats of arms are recorded of all the thousands of French noblemen killed by the English in the Battle of Agincourt in 1415. Outside the Citadel the elegant Château de Montreuil now serves as a sumptuous hotel.

Montreuil has been on the beaten track for a long time, and was always a popular stopping place on the road to Paris. Now, tourists are sufficiently numerous that some of the cafés and restaurants have signs in English and there's even a Hotel Shakespeare. But Victor Hugo, rather than Shakespeare, is the writer most associated with Montreuil. The town fascinated him and he used it as the setting for key scenes in *Les Misérables*.

Citadel open daily (excluding Tue.) a.m. and p.m.; closed Oct. Hôtel Dieu chapel open July–Aug. p.m. only; rest of year see contact address on door

ARGOULES
On D192, 58 km south of Boulogne and 95 km from Calais

A succession of wide, verdant valleys flows westward out of Picardy into the Channel. South of Montreuil and the Canche, the more rustic Authie meanders towards the sea. On its bank, little Argoules is no more than a single row of cottages and houses, mostly painted white, half-hidden behind masses of flowers in pots and gardens. The last buildings in the village are a prosperous little manor house and a useful two-star hotel and restaurant, called the Gros Tilleul, standing beneath the branches of the great *tilleul* (lime tree) itself. Behind the dwellings spreads a cool, delightful water meadow with trees, running alongside the river. It's a place for the most leisurely of walks, or for idle relaxation.

The manor house

Although there are no shops, an odd assortment of things can be bought here: fishing permits, high-class antiques, wine direct from the producer. And houses – several are for sale.

But there is something more to Argoules. At the other end of the village, a dignified stone gateway leads into a large enclosed formal garden and courtyard. Along its far side extends a handsome grey edifice under a dark slate roof, austere but for the ivy clinging to its walls. This is the former Cistercian abbey of Valloires. Although a fine example of eighteenth-century architecture, the abbey dates back to the twelfth century, having been founded by a family of the local nobility. In 1346, after the battle between the English and French at nearby Crécy (see below), many of the bodies of the slaughtered French noblemen were brought here.

Years passed and the abbey prospered, but in the 1740s and 1750s the ancient buildings suffered a succession of fires, and the monks replaced them with the present château-like building. Late in the nineteenth century, a community of Basiliens took up residence here. Like the original Cistercians, the Basiliens were monks who advocated a life of hard work and long prayer, but wore a blue uniform of ordinary shirts, hats and trousers instead of robes. Today the abbey has been taken over as a children's remand home, yet is open for visits. The interior still has its excellent baroque decoration.

Continue along the lane beyond the abbey to the neighbouring hamlet of Petit-Preaux, where the big, wooden wheel of a working water mill turns in the stream of the River Authie. A tiny bridge crosses the water here, and beside it the Bar du Vieux Moulin serves snacks and drinks on a riverside terrace and lawn.

Abbey of Valloires open for guided visits April–early Nov., a.m. and p.m.

Valloires abbey

CRÉCY-EN-PONTHIEU
On D12, 70 km south of Boulogne and 107 km from Calais

The great battlefield of Crécy is just fields of grain and vegetables today. Attractive, rolling farm country dotted with leafy woods reaches away to north and east, while the treetops of the Forest of Crécy cover higher ground to the south and west.

On 26 August 1346, the forces of France and England clashed on that field at the battle of Crécy. It was one of the first, and one of the bloodiest encounters in the century of war between the two countries over the future of France, whose crown and half its land had passed, through marriage and inheritance, to Edward III of England. The French nobility had decided to fight for French rule under Edward's second cousin Philippe de Valois.

Edward III arrived at Crécy with 20,000 English, Irish and Welsh soldiers. Facing him was Philippe with 60,000 men, tired from the march. The French and their allies threw themselves robustly into the fight, but were subject to a ceaseless slaughter due to three things they had not expected: disciplined soldiers obeying orders, skilled archers and – perhaps for the first time in Europe – cannon. According to reports of the time, the French were 'awed by the rigid stillness of the English ranks, who let fly their arrows so thick it seemed like snow'. Not only that, but the French had the sun in their eyes. The utterly convincing English victory was to mark the course of the conflict and set the tone of the Hundred Years War, even though eventually the French were to succeed and reclaim their crown.

Jean de Luxembourg, the courageous and revered old king of Bohemia, who was leading the French troops, fell beside his son in the battle. The Croix de Bohème (Cross of Bohemia), by the D56 southeast of Crécy, marks the spot where they died.

Modern Crécy is a large village, quiet and unremarkable. Its wide *rue principale* serves as a shopping centre for this rural area. From the lower end of the village, near the bank of the River Maye, rises the spire of an ornate and fortified Gothic church in grey stone. Close by, Virginia creeper drapes an inviting hotel-restaurant, Hôtel de la Maye, where locals enjoy leisurely Sunday lunches. Walk up from the river to Place Jean de Luxembourg at one end of the busy main street. Not only is the square named for him, but it also contains a stone memorial to the brave Bohemian, 'and his valiant companions, who fell for France in the Battle of Crécy'. Strangely, this was erected as recently as 1905.

At the other end of the little *place* is a memorial much older, the brick 'lantern', tall and slender and encircled by flowers, put up in 1189 by no less a person than Eleanor of Aquitaine. The dowry Eleanor brought on her marriage to Henry II of England – about one-third the area of France

The Villages of Northern France

was hers – set the stage for the centuries of conflict which culminated in the Hundred Years War. The inscription on the lantern describes her as 'Queen of England and Countess of Ponthieu', and explains that it is 'in memory of her sons Richard Cœur de Lion and John Lackland, who have gone in the Third Crusade to the Holy Land'. The fact that they were not dead at the time shows the view people took of the crusades and of such a journey.

Continue through the village to the other side, and leave on D111 to find, 1 kilometre away, the hilltop site of Edward III's windmill (signposted Moulin Edouard III). The mill itself has gone, but the view that Edward contemplated from this higher ground remains. The mill was chosen to be the English stronghold if the battle went against them.

South of the site, the Forêt de Crécy is crossed by pleasant paths and lanes among the trees. Beyond lies the next of Picardy's valleys, the Somme.

LE CROTOY
Off D940, 20 km west of Abbeville and 105 km from Calais

Between the Somme Bay and the Authie Bay – two huge river estuaries on the coast of Picardy – extends a vast expanse of reclaimed marsh, mostly now covered with wheat fields and rough pastures. Clean sea air and a huge changing sky blow, inspiring and invigorating, across this immense plain beside the Channel. Along the northern shore of the Somme Bay where it turns into the sea, a terrain of sand dunes and marsh has been preserved as the Parc Ornithologique du Marquenterre, a sanctuary for a multitude of bird species which thrive here.

Marshy, sandy salt meadows, cut across by narrow water channels, continue right around the Somme Bay from north to south, and are called in the local dialect *mollières*. On these salty pastures – *prés salés* – sheep are put out to graze, and their meat is a speciality in this otherwise very fishy area of coast and river. Cattle graze too, and horses wander at liberty.

For miles the traveller must continue across this flat landscape to reach Le Crotoy, on the north shore of the

Somme estuary. Only two roads go in or out of this small fishing town, and both run straight through it to the quayside.

The quay runs alongside the mouth of the tidal Somme, at low tide a huge sheet of mudflats, edged with sand, and at high tide an expanse of water on which fishing trawlers set out to sea. Men work at boats pulled up on the sandy margin. Birds fly in hundreds over the river and flats, or swim in the water. The thin shrill sound of seagulls, sometimes melancholy and plaintive, sometimes joyous and excited, hangs always in the air. Far away on the other side of the estuary, tiny in the distance, St-Valery-sur-Somme can be seen to the south, and the lighthouse at Le Hourdel to the west.

Oysters can be bought from open air stalls on the quayside, and jostling yachts are tied up prettily in a small harbour. River and mudflats almost encircle the village, imparting their own peace and silence to its streets. Houses are simple, brick, many of them painted white and decorated with colourful window boxes.

The Somme estuary

However, in contrast, Le Crotoy's main street is bustling, noisy and alive, with a great array of little shops and even an amusement arcade. The street starts from a statue of Jeanne d'Arc on the waterfront, unusual in portraying her not so much as a soldier, but more as a woman. Jeanne was held briefly at Le Crotoy before being taken across the bay to St-Valery, thence for trial and execution in Rouen. Le Crotoy was in those days a heavily fortified harbour, and she was imprisoned in its now-vanished castle.

A reminder of those medieval defenses can be found just off the main street, at Le Crotoy's small church. Though Gothic, and made of dressed stone, the building is stocky and gaunt, and fortified in the most functional way – it looks almost like a wartime bunker. Inside, the ceiling is rib-vaulted but with remarkable simplicity, and made of bricks. As a measure of Le Crotoy's decline from important harbour to quiet little fishing town, a memorial to those who died in the Second World War names only six men (three described as *marins*, sailors), while the list of those who fell in the First World War numbers more than forty. Models of seagoing vessels in full sail hang in one of the aisles, and a fishing net encloses the choir. It's clear enough how important fishing and the sea have been to the people of Le Crotoy.

Somme Bay railway: steam and diesel trains run around the Somme Bay from Le Crotoy to St-Valery, a return journey of one and a half hours. Open May–Sept. on Sun. and fêtes; also Sat. July–Sept.; also Wed. and Thur. July–Aug.

ST-VALERY-SUR-SOMME
Just off D940, 18 km west of Abbeville and 120 km from Calais

On the south shore of the Somme estuary, with a channel of river passing alongside its quay, St-Valery is a modern town and an ancient village. In the water, fishermen stand up to their knees, even to their waists, and in a sectioned-off port fishing trawlers are moored waiting for higher tide. A few motor cruisers and yachts, too, are tied. Beyond a sandbank extend the broad mudflats of the Somme Bay, and in the distance the white houses of Le Crotoy catch the light. Seagulls wheel and cry in the vast openness above the Bay.

The riverside roadway is delightfully traffic free, effectively a promenade. Shaded with plane and lime trees, it makes an enjoyable walk. Join the promenade at its start, beside the Calvaire des Marins near the centre of the busy, larger *ville basse*. Continue some five hundred paces until there is a left turn. Take this turning, passing a big seafood restaurant, and find on the right a steep cobbled lane, Rue de la Porte de Nevers, which winds up to enter the covered fourteenth-century Porte de Nevers into the *ville haute*, the older part of town. The name of the gateway is a reminder that St-Valery became a possession of the Dukes of Nevers in the seventeenth century.

At once the noise of traffic dies away, as silence and a sense of the past sweeps over the street. Pass through the gateway to enter a small cobbled square. Ahead is the black and white chequered wall of the Gothic church of St Martin. A covered alley of cobbles leads off, burrowing beneath a timbered house and behind the back wall of the church to emerge into an open cobbled terrace on the edge of the old town's high fortifications. From its parapet the

The church in St-Valery's ville haute

view – a little obscured by the leafy top branches of tall trees growing below – embraces the river, the whole of the Somme Bay and the Marquenterre beyond.

Continue round to the gaunt main entrance of the church, which resembles that of Le Crotoy on the other side of the bay. Inside here, too, a fishing net around the choir tells of St-Valery's ancient preoccupation. Walk further into the *ville haute* to arrive at the old town's other entrance, the more imposing twelfth-century gateway flanked by towers, the Porte de Guillaume. It has a magnificent view across the Somme Bay and out to sea.

South of St-Valery the countryside begins to take on the look of Upper Normandy's Caux region – high, open fields – and the next valley, the Bresle, marks the Duchy's frontier. To remain in Picardy, turn back towards the River Somme, by-passing Abbeville.

Somme Bay railway: see details under Le Crotoy, page 34

LONG
On D32 and D112, 15 km east of Abbeville and 131 km from Calais

Although the name Somme evokes tragic memories, the river itself, broad and leisurely in its wide valley, conveys only a quiet sense of peace and contentment. The country road which follows its north bank often looks over the lush foliage which crowds close to the waterside. Along the valley workaday rural villages and small towns – plain, brick-built, often reconstructed after wartime damage – have their own modest charm. They are indeed a testimony to the endurance of the countryside and country people.

Long, lying at the foot of a gentle slope, follows the side of the river, which is concealed here by thick woods. The village has an elegant little Louis XV château, a handsome building of brick and white stone behind very high gates which reveal a formal courtyard and lawn. It's a privately owned *monument classé*, still lived in.

The village rises around the wall of the château grounds. The old parish church was successfully rebuilt in its Gothic style, and has kept the original tall sixteenth-century spire. As you drive north away from the village and the river, it

*Long's château
beside the Somme*
can still be seen rising out of the land when all the rest of
Long has disappeared from view.

Château open for guided visits in Aug. and Sept. by arrangement

ST-RIQUIER
On D925 and D32, 9 km northeast of Abbeville and 122 km from Calais

Tractors and hay lorries pass by or park alongside the
simple brick houses of this big farming village. Fields,
orchards and pasture with grazing cows penetrate almost
into the centre. A disused railway track passing through has
become green and overgrown. At the plain little main
square, Place de 11-Novembre, two busy D roads intersect,
yet there's an air of remoteness.

St-Riquier is no ordinary crossroads community. Beside
the *place*, a magnificent flamboyant Gothic church looks out
across a paved square. A multitude of statuary – the soft
pale stone damaged by war and revolution, and simply by

37

the weather – adorns a richly carved façade. Its high tower, ornate and white, rises far above the roof-tops. This is the church of a celebrated Benedictine abbey, founded 1,600 years ago, visited by Charlemagne, and a great centre of piety and pilgrimage for centuries.

It suffered numerous attacks, by Normans, English and Germans, which took their toll at last, though local people fought ferociously to protect the abbey. In 1536, the destructive soldiers of Holy Roman Emperor Charles V came here and were humiliated when the village women proved too much for them. The heroine of that battle was one Becquétoille, who – legend records – with her bare hands killed the Emperor's standard bearer and destroyed his flag.

The present lavish church dates from the fifteenth and sixteenth centuries (though parts are two centuries older). Inside, there is yet more elaborate decoration and carving, and ceilings superbly vaulted. The abbey treasury is especially interesting, its walls painted with a strange picture of *The Three Dead and The Three Living*.

St-Riquier's abbey church dominates the village

The other abbey buildings, around the side and back of the church, were rebuilt in the seventeenth century and today contain a départemental cultural centre, restaurant and a local museum of rural life. They form a fine ensemble of pale stone. There are attractive gardens too, and a great variety of concerts is held here, ranging from classical to jazz to steel bands.

On the other side of the main square stands a substantial five-storey tower, once a grim medieval fortification but now housing a clock at the top, a tourist office at the bottom, and made pretty with window boxes. Today it is locally known as the *Beffroi* (belfry). Five hundred years ago Jeanne d'Arc, on her way to face the ecclesiastical court at Rouen, was locked inside the tower, where she was visited by the monks.

A detail of the church's flamboyant façade

Abbey church treasury open for guided visits Mon.–Fri. a.m. and p.m., excluding Tue., and Sun. p.m. Museum open May–Nov., Mon.–Fri. p.m., Sat.–Sun. a.m. and p.m.; but June–Sept. daily a.m. and p.m.

EASTERN PICARDY

The River Oise is a great divide in eastern Picardy. On its right bank, the country has been scarred by wartime destruction, industry and agriculture on a large scale. Yet on its left bank lie magnificent, unspoiled beech forests, agreeable villages and historic towns. This combination is nothing new. When the young Robert Louis Stevenson paddled down the Oise in 1876, he, too, noted the contrast of smoking, glowing manufactories with rustic farming country and woodland. Our village route takes the left bank!

In early days this was the first foothold of the Franks, that Germanic tribe whose chiefs were to become the kings of France, and whose mispronounced Latin was to become the French language. Seeing that the Roman hold on this territory had become weak, in the year 406 the Franks invaded. By 486, when Clovis defeated the Romans at Soissons, they had pushed aside the Roman colonists. In the century which followed, new dioceses and abbeys – centres of wealth, art and learning – were established under Frankish rule across eastern Picardy. The Franks asserted themselves with ease over the other Germanic tribes which had attempted to carve power bases out of the collapsed Roman Empire. In 768, at Noyon, on the banks of the Oise, Charlemagne had himself crowned King of France; and in 800, at Rome, Emperor of the Holy Roman Empire.

Charlemagne, a giant among history's kings and statesmen, created order and a sense of moral purpose out of the dark chaos left by the fall of Rome. His military conquests virtually created both France and Germany. Yet he remained a staunch Frankish patriot, devoted to the region of northern France which had become the home of his people.

During the Middle Ages, the region prospered, and was a little less troubled by war than Artois and western Picardy, where the conflict between England and France was being more fiercely played out. In later centuries, and in modern times too, although the whole of northern France suffered in war, as the countless cemeteries of the Commonwealth War Graves Commission bear testimony, this eastern flank of Picardy did not see the worst of it.

Although there are signs of the damage done, fortunately many fine historic buildings managed to survive the two world wars. Renaissance and Gothic masterpieces can be found in the small towns. Gothic architecture in particular developed early here, and many towns and villages preserve interesting first attempts to use the new style. Many date back to the twelfth century. Some of Europe's oldest and best examples of the transition to Gothic can be found in these towns of Picardy, especially in the cathedrals of Laon and Noyon.

Laon (pronounced as if the 'a' were absent) crowns a steep hill which lifts it high above the surrounding country. One of the most fascinating towns in Picardy, it has a long history. The Gauls had a settlement here, which was taken over by the Romans, who fortified it; later, after the Franks had established themselves in this region, Laon became their royal residence. For over 1,200 years, from 497 onwards, it was also the seat of an influential bishopric. Inevitably, it was the objective of many invaders, and witnessed much fighting and destruction. During the Hundred Years War and in both of the world wars, Laon was pounded. Yet it survived with most of its character and appearance unscathed.

Old Laon is the *ville haute*, or upper town, and contains a wealth of interest within its encircling ramparts. The shape of the town, following the topography of the hill summit, divides it into two districts: La Cité and Le Bourg. Both preserve a superb array of historic buildings. There are two Gothic churches built when the style was new. The handsome church of St Martin dates back to 1150. Laon's high point, literally and metaphorically, is its magnificent cathedral built about 1160. In the lofty, pale interior, a plaque recalls 'One million dead of the British Empire who fell in the Great War... and of whom the greater part rest in France'.

Ten kilometres west of the Oise, the historic hilltop town of St-Quentin overlooks the River Somme. In this

Among the forests of eastern Picardy: the château at Pierrefonds

century the town has expanded well past its ancient limits, marked by today's encircling boulevards. It took a heavy beating during both world wars, especially in 1918 during the Second Battle of the Somme which was focused on the town. Yet its greatest buildings survived and have been carefully restored. A magnificent cathedral stands at its heart. Built during the thirteenth to fifteenth centuries, it represents the culmination of pure Gothic taste, and is one of the loveliest French buildings of the period. See too the flamboyant *hôtel de ville* (town hall) of 1509 in the main square. Musée Lécuyer, a few yards away in Rue Antoine Lécuyer, displays arts and antiquities, including a collection of pastels by the eighteenth-century portraitist Quentin Delatour (or La Tour, as he is sometimes known).

Noyon, a short distance south, now a quiet, provincial market town, was for centuries a city of importance. In 768 Charlemagne was crowned here, and its cathedral of 1150 was the first in France to be built in the Gothic style. As such it interestingly combines Romanesque and Gothic themes. Inside, its three long aisles and three stories of arches have exquisite elegance. Lying west of the Oise, and not far from the Somme, the town suffered extensively during the Great War. The cathedral, all but destroyed, had to be painstakingly reconstructed, only to come under very heavy bombardment again in 1940. Once more, it was faithfully repaired.

Protestant reformer Jean Calvin was born at Noyon in 1509 and lived here until about eleven years old. The ornate *hôtel de ville*, dating from the fifteenth century, is a fine example of a medieval town hall. Robert Louis Stevenson stopped at Noyon on his paddling voyage through northern France and although impressed by the cathedral, he summed up the town as 'but a stack of brown roofs at best, where I believe people live very respectably in a quiet way'. He might say the same today.

Perhaps the most enjoyable town to visit in eastern Picardy is Compiègne. It lies mainly on the left bank of the Oise, which at this point has become wide and stately. The main attraction of the town is the triangular Royal Palace, its serene Petit Parc, and the glorious forest which touches the town. For centuries this was a rural retreat of French kings, though the present grandiose palace only dates from the eighteenth century. As soon as royalty had been disposed of, Napoleon took up residence here. A tour of the *appartements* reveals that Napoleon (and Napoleon III who lived here after him) were very fond of ugly and ostentatious decor and furnishings. Included on the tour is a museum of vintage motor vehicles.

The centre of Compiègne has a good deal of charm, and an air of prosperity and good living. Among several historic buildings, don't miss the ornate Gothic town hall in the main square, Place de l'Hôtel de Ville. Its façade is a mass of stonework and carving, and at the top a bizarre mechanical clock has little figures called *picantins* ringing out the quarter-hours. The *hôtel de ville* contains an unusual collection of tin soldiers, laid out in reconstructions of great battles, while next door, the Musée Vivenel houses a priceless collection of classical Greek vases. Every Saturday, a colourful market fills the square in front of the building.

All these towns of Picardy, and many of the villages, have good restaurants. Hearty soups and stews are a speciality. *Soupe des Hortillons*, for example, is a substantial vegetable stew, appropriate in a region noted for its huge fields of carrots, cabbages and cauliflowers. Strongly flavoured meat dishes, tripe, *pâtés* and spicy sausages are popular too, as is local game from the forests, such as pheasant, quail and hare. Cheeseboards feature the strong, tangy cheeses of Picardy and Flanders. Beer is often an ingredient in the local dishes, and some people enjoy one of the palatable local beers with their food instead of wine.

The Villages of Northern France

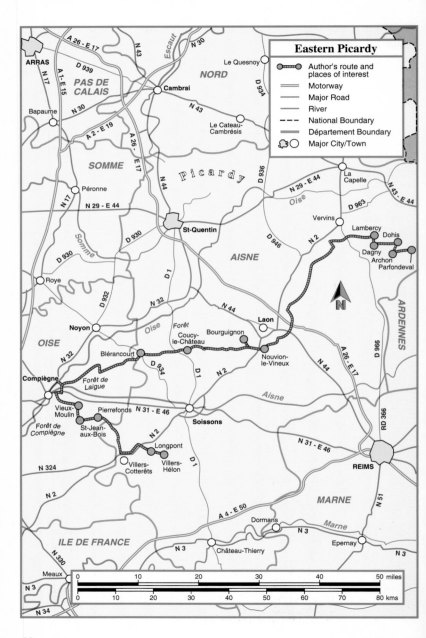

PARFONDEVAL
On D520, 45 km northeast of Laon and 146 km from Calais

None of Picardy is truly border country. To the north, French Flanders protects it, while to the east lie Champagne and the French Ardennes. Yet one tiny corner of Picardy does touch the frontier. Although the length of border amounts to barely 10 kilometres, this northeastern district of Picardy – called la Thièrache – as a result suffered frequent attack throughout the centuries.

It was a jewel well worth seizing, or protecting. In the Thièrache, a myriad of streams water a profoundly rural, green and varied landscape. A great number of small farming communities work productive fields, gardens, orchards and pastures. Countless little lanes, with hardly any traffic other than tractors, thread from one attractive village to another.

A fine example of a Thièrache fortified village church, Parfondeval

In the violent past, the farms and manor houses, sometimes even cottages, but most especially the churches (which acted as refuges for the whole population in time of danger) were built with simple fortifications, which today often appear more charming than daunting.

At Parfondeval, most houses are substantial red-brick dwellings under black slate roofs, with an air of well-to-do dignity. Yet this is a simple farm village, attractively arranged around a central green with tall trees and a pond. Farmyards – muddy enclosures with hens, tractors, trailers, milk churns – reach to the village green.

*Cottage brickwork
of the Thièrache*

Beyond one end of the green, the sixteenth-century church rises up as a veritable fortress, surrounded by a wall and houses which line up as if to defend it. An archway (with a small dwelling above) gives entrance to the enclosure, within which the church has a hexagonal spire and two massive round towers, topped with pointed black conical turrets. It looks like a miniature fortress, undecorated but for twin white stone portals in Renaissance style. In keeping with its impressively defensive aspect, the church door may be locked, although pinned to it is the name of the person with the key.

ARCHON
On D744 and D620, 43 km northeast of Laon and 137 km from Calais

In this undulating, uneven Thièrache countryside, with streams twisting about among small hills, covered with rough, unkempt pasture, the villages seem to lie half-concealed. Mature, overgrown hedges separate the fields.

In contrast to the slight air of prosperity among Parfondeval's sturdy dwellings, Archon is a rustic cluster of cottages, some of brick, some of wattle and daub, a good many in a state of crumbling disrepair, and under black slate roofs that likewise could do with some maintenance. A simple, hard-working community, Archon has farmyards and barns extending right into the centre. Milk churns await collection outside the front doors.

The centre of the village consists of little more than a triangular space made by the meeting of lanes. At just that point stands a rather odd building, a small fortress of brick standing on a base of large stones. It could be a miniature château or tiny manor house. In reality this is the village church. Ponderously fortified, gaunt, undecorated, the building has two huge round towers on either side of the doorway. Between the towers, a balcony served as a lookout post. Inside, the bare walls and simple atmosphere of the single nave suggest a humble, unassuming parish.

DOHIS
On D61, 45 km northeast of Laon and 143 km from Calais

Half a dozen of the Thièrache lanes meet in Dohis. The small village is hardly more than a single row of picturesque, brick and timber farmhouses and their wooden barns set back beyond wide, green verges dotted with flowers. At one end of the row a battered church and equally long-suffering *mairie*, both made of weatherworn, red brick and stone, stand side by side. The church is entered through an arched, brick porch, vestige of simple defenses added to the building in the seventeenth century. The church itself is much older, with parts of the nave dating from the twelfth century.

A slate-roofed *lavoir* near the church still has running water, and local women still come here with their washing. Walk or drive uphill beyond the church for a superb view of the village in its bucolic setting above the stream of the Brume.

DAGNY-LAMBERCY

On D61, 41 km northeast of Laon and 137 km from Calais

A village of barns and farmyards, with little traffic but tractors hauling hay or milking equipment, there is nothing more to Dagny than a few attractive houses of old brick and timber, a wonderfully quiet, rural atmosphere and a beautiful setting among rolling fields and copses. Farms come right into the village centre. Neatly trimmed grass verges run up from the road to the buildings under their uneven, grey roofs. One house appears to have been fortified, another has a farmyard enclosed within imposing walls and a covered gateway. Within, cows eat hay from a manger. The church here, too, is brick and stone which has been repaired several times. In its graveyard a Commonwealth War Grave stands among the others.

A fortified farm in the village centre

Lambercy, standing quite separate just a few hundred metres along the road, has now become part of the same *commune*. It is another old-fashioned hamlet of simple brick and timber farmhouses, with muddy yards and gardens beside them. Stand here an hour before dinner and you'll see people come out to gather their vegetables for the evening meal. Fields of cows come together in the village street, and there's an old *lavoir* still in use.

Continue along any Thièrache lane to find yet another peaceful, rustic village dominated by its fortified church. Beyond Dagny, the white Romanesque church in the village of Hary, the heavily defended sixteenth-century church at Burelles, and the massive square tower which guards the barrack-like church of Prisces, all deserve a leisurely pause.

Southward, the Thièrache gives way to flatter landscapes, but another 20 kilometres on country roads reaches the satisfying scenery around Laon.

NOUVION-LE-VINEUX
On D25, 8 km from Laon and 190 km from Calais

Just south of the impressive old hilltop town of Laon lies a comfortably unkempt countryside of little hills and dales, woods, rough pasture and orchards. This is the Montagne de Laon, though the name merely suggests a contrast with the flatness of the rest of the region: the highest summit in the Montagne reaches only 180 metres.

In these modest hills many lovely old village churches can be found. On some roads, almost every village has a simple parish church of note. Many date from the twelfth and thirteenth centuries. Along the D25, for example, several peaceful small villages and hamlets have remarkable churches.

Nouvion is one of them. At the entrance to the village, water still flows in a wooden channel through a small, wooden *lavoir* with its date, 1841, hanging in large figures. Continue to a little village green with trees arranged in a circle. From here a street climbs to a basic Gothic church built as early as the twelfth century. Through a covered porch, the interior has no decoration but for carved capitals on tall and slender columns. All in pale stone, almost unadorned, it possesses a humble, austere elegance.

BOURGUIGNON
Just off D5 and D65, 8 km from Laon and 190 km from Calais

In the midst of the delightful rusticity of the Montagne de Laon, the village of Bourguignon preserves an unexpected elegance and style. Its narrow lanes form a circle of handsome pale stone houses, some old, some new, many of

A country mansion of Bourguignon

them substantial dwellings with walled gardens. A few could even pass for châteaux. Bushes and creepers grow in profusion. The whole village is a conservation area.

Outside the village on the north side, a narrow lane heads up to Les Cruettes, troglodyte caves in an eminence of land. From here the view takes in the town of Laon and the Montagne. (The viewpoint is signposted *Panorama des Cruettes*.) On the south side of Bourguignon, its neighbouring village Royaucourt has a fine thirteenth-century Gothic church with flying buttresses.

The whole area evokes the work of the Le Nain brothers, Antoine, Louis and Mathieu, distinguished painters of the seventeenth century whose scenes of country life are considered the high point of French realism of the period. Born in Laon, and living in Bourguignon, the three artists derived most of their inspiration from this rural scene.

COUCY-LE-CHÂTEAU
Just off D1, 43 km northeast of Compiègne and 230 km from Calais

During the Middle Ages the great château of Coucy, the largest and most magnificent castle in Europe, was the very symbol of feudal power. Yet its lords were not kings or dukes, as their motto proudly declared: *Roys ne suis, ni prince, ni duc, ni comte aussi. Je suis le sire de Coucy.*

Built in the thirteenth century, the castle was constructed on a monumental scale as if for giants. Even the staircases rose in huge steps too big for normal men. And the lords of Coucy were, in their way, giants among men. The life they lived was of a fantastic extravagance, their influence far-reaching, their dinner guests the most powerful figures in Christendom. In 1652, when their domain was finally taken into the monarchy of France, the château was largely dismantled, though even that task proved impossible and much remained standing. The end came at last in 1917, when German troops set about deliberately destroying the legendary castle. Yet even they were unable to erase this mighty landmark from Europe's history. The immense fragments which remain are still impressive.

Do not linger in the modern area at the foot of the hill but straight away follow signs to the *ville haute* (upper town). If arriving from Laon on D5, you pass into the upper town through the narrow Porte de Laon. Towers and walls enclose the *ville haute*, an atmospheric fortified village which kept its medieval character until the German attack of 1917. Now everything is either restored or new, houses of pale stone clustered together, yet still with many picturesque corners and cobbled pavements.

The whole of the walled town once formed part of the château – a kind of huge servants' quarters. The lordly part of the castle lay through another superb, fortified gateway; to reach it, follow signs to the château for about 100 metres from Place de l'Hôtel de Ville. Within the gates lies a large, open space, the former *basse cour* or courtyard, and remnants of the lofty château itself, from which there is an excellent view. The Germans left nothing of the keep, though. Inside a fine gatehouse at the entrance to the *cour*, a permanent exhibition, including a fascinating scale model of the

Coucy: once the largest castle in Europe

medieval castle, keep and town, gives a clear impression of the drama and history of Coucy.

Passing through Porte de Chauny, descend by the lower town. Beside the road, the château walls seem to rise sheer out of the rock. Leaving Coucy, the road soon penetrates the attractive Basse-Forêt de Coucy, a dense, deciduous woodland. In 1918 these trees concealed the huge Paris Gun which bombarded the French capital, some 120 kilometres away.

Château and museum open daily excluding Tue. in winter

BLÉRANCOURT
On D934 and D6, 31 km northeast of Compiègne and 217 km from Calais

Leaving Coucy forest, the road (D934) crosses high, open countryside, alternating patches of woodland and large arable fields, at length reaching this unassuming small town. Among the first sights to greet travellers is the rather grand gateway of a seventeenth-century orphanage, a splendid building in pale stone with a hexagonal clocktower. At the centre of town, prominent at a junction of modest streets, the *hôtel de ville* stands on top of an arcaded, covered market of pale stone.

Only a few paces from the *hôtel de ville*, Blérancourt reveals its little gem. You first come to a green bordered by trees. Around this, and through its centre, run cobbled roadways, giving access to the gateway of a seventeenth-century Renaissance château. Walk through to discover a formal palace garden, perfectly tended, neatly clipped and precise: the trimmed yew trees look like carvings standing on a green rug. All that survives of the château are two single-storey pavilions separated by an archway. Originally much larger, this was the palace of the Dukes of Gesvres, but was taken over at the Revolution and largely dismantled. The two wings today house an unusual museum, mostly of Americana, devoted to Franco-American co-operation.

Beside the main gateway of the château, the Hostellerie le Griffon is a solid, old *auberge* draped in greenery. It's a tempting sight, a comfortable provincial hotel with a good restaurant.

Continuing west and south, the road (D130) soon re-enters fine woodland, the forests of Ourscamps (the abbey of Ourscamps stands just 7 kilometres from the road, on the bank of the Oise) and Laigue. The Forêt de Laigue is

The château gateway, with auberge alongside

bounded on the south by the broad River Aisne, which the road crosses at its confluence with the Oise. The Oise, further enlarged by these new waters, at once flows into the pleasant royal town of Compiègne.

Château and Museum open daily excluding Tue. (p.m. only in winter)

VIEUX-MOULIN
On D85, 10 km east of Compiègne and 229 km from Calais

The Forêt de Compiègne is a glorious expanse, some 14,500 hectares of fine old woodland crisscrossed with tracks and paths. Although largely flat, it does possess some hilly areas, making the scene even more enjoyable. Almost entirely deciduous, mainly beech, the forest appears as a dense mass of green foliage and unkempt undergrowth growing freely in disordered profusion. This is a last vestige of the original woodland which in ancient times cloaked the entire landscape from the Seine to the Ardennes.

Vieux-Moulin's curious church

It has a long history as a royal playground, where the French monarchy, during their sojourns at the palace of Compiègne, would ride or hunt. Today it is a popular place for picnics and weekend walks. The forest margins lie within the town boundary of Compiègne. Leave the roads and the larger tracks, though, and it is easy enough to slip away from any trace of other people. Then the sense of peace and tranquillity is astonishing.

Quaint, old-fashioned fingerposts, tall and white, sign every meeting of paths, tracks and roads. Here and there, a few houses can be glimpsed within the forest, and even villages – indeed, there's a bus service that serves the forest residents. One such village is the superbly situated, and in every way delightful, Vieux-Moulin.

At its fringes, trees conceal well-to-do houses, old and new. Grassy verges and lovely stone cottages line the lane into the village centre. Though very tranquil, this is a proper working village. And although exceptionally pretty, it hasn't been prettified. At its heart stands a remarkable, little church, with a broad, arcaded porch of wood and stone. The church is of pale stone, but its square belfry, rising in two stages with curiously wide eaves, is tiled with wood and black slate. The whole effect is distinctly oriental.

However, opposite the church is something thoroughly French: an enchanting old inn, the Auberge du Daguet, adorned with clinging Virginia creeper and window boxes overflowing with colour. The auberge is in part a good restaurant and in part a simple village bar. Inside, old beams give a suitably solid, rustic appearance. From here, all roads lead straight back into the forest: a perfect little place in a lovely setting.

ST-JEAN-AUX-BOIS
On D85, 11 km southeast of Compiègne and 230 km from Calais

Hidden away within the Compiègne forest, tiny St-Jean 'in the woods' has a surprising air of normality, as if unaware of its surroundings. Like Vieux-Moulin, it has not been artificially prettified, yet its simple, sturdy cottages of stone blocks, many of them single storey, have a natural appeal.

The name of the bar at its centre, Bistrot des Solitaires, is a sort of wordplay, since the village was once called La Solitude – quite reasonably. The bistro stands on a miniature crossroads of turnings that go nowhere. One of them, Rue des Meuniers leads to the forest in just a few paces; along here there's a good 3-star hotel-restaurant, whimsically called À la Bonne Idée, a tempting little place in a fine old building. Opposite Rue des Meuniers, an old stone bridge, stepping over a stream which forms part of a miniature moat, leads through a fortified gateway into the enclosed grounds of a former abbey.

The domain of the twelfth-century abbey has become part of the village, with terraces of charming little dwellings now given suitably monastic street names, such as Rue des Abbesses or Rue du Couvent. Some hung with leafy vines, and with flower beds at their feet, the cottages form a defensive ring around the church and grounds. *La grand cour* is hardly more than a green and pleasant churchyard, full of polled lime trees gathered around a large old chestnut.

The thirteenth-century church, a lovely example of early Gothic work, is all that remains of the abbey, which for 500 years was occupied by Benedictines, then for a century by Augustines before falling into disuse. Today it is just the parish church of St-Jean-aux-Bois, with a small, walled graveyard beside it. The church is entered through a little courtyard at the side of the building. The elegant, harmonious interior has little decoration, being a single nave of unadorned white stone, and like the village itself conveys an air of calm simplicity. Yet somehow there is also something majestic in the height and proportions.

St-Jean makes an excellent starting point – or rest place – for walks and rides through the beech trees. Several tracks suitable for cycling lead away from the village. At the end of Rue des Meuniers a signboard map shows the cycle routes of the whole forest.

PIERREFONDS
On D973, 14 km southeast of Compiègne and 233 km from Calais

An immense, imposing castle in pale grey stone, in perfect condition with huge round towers and delicate pointed turrets, ringed by a high, defensive parapet indented with castellations, stands proudly on its leafy hillside. From a rocky ledge it looms over a bustling village of fine old houses gathered at the foot of the castle walls, on the shore of a tranquil lake. Trees plunge steeply down on every side right into the streets.

In this superb woodland setting in the fringes of Compiègne forest, the village of Pierrefonds possesses an air of dignity. Natural springs at the lakeside gave it pretentions as a small spa; that, together with the presence of aristocracy on the hill, once made Pierrefonds a favoured resort of the rich, the famous and the noble.

Everything here still seems to have style and taste: even the post office has a gable façade of beautiful cut stone grandly carved with the words *Postes Telegraphe Telephone* above the crest of Pierrefonds. The lake, with its ducks and geese sailing among water lilies, is surrounded by handsome trees, in the shade of which café and restaurant tables invite leisurely hours on covered terraces. Those on the north bank have the better view, across a corner of lake, over the village centre, and up to the massive bulk of the royal château on its hill.

Ornamental yet also defensive, the castle has served well as both palace and fortress. The site was originally fortified in the twelfth century. The present building was constructed in 1390 by Charles VI who gave it to his brother Louis d'Orléans who was assasinated in 1407 by his cousin Jean-sans-Peur, the powerful duke of Burgundy. The mighty castle then successfully withstood seiges by the English, the

Mighty Pierrefonds's château rising above the village

Burgundians and four times by French royal troops, before coming into the grasp of the crown and being partly dismantled in 1617. The building was ignominiously sold at the Revolution, but managed to survive relatively unharmed, and in 1813 was purchased by Napoleon (the price was only 3,000 F). Fifty years later, Napoleon III asked Viollet-le-Duc to restore the castle to its former grandeur, and although doubts have been raised as to the historical authenticity of his work, the result is one of the most impressive and handsome medieval fortresses surviving in France.

From Place de l'Hôtel de Ville, the main square in Pierrefonds, walk up the steep path that leads to the *route charretière*, which encircles the palace. Enter on the south side across a drawbridge, through the fortified main gateway beside Caesar's Tower (in which Napoleon had his bedroom) and the splendid *donjon* or keep. The keep's interior gives a good idea of the comforts and hardships of a life of lordly luxury in medieval times. Within the walls is the great Court of Honour, enclosed by the castle's halls, barracks, chapel and apartments. Most of the château is open to the public, and there's a permanent exhibition on the life and work of Viollet-le-Duc, that ubiquitous military historian and architect, tireless builder (and restorer) of fortresses and fortifications along the frontiers of France.

Château open daily 1000–1115, 1400–1715, excluding fêtes and Tue. (and Wed. in winter)

LONGPONT
On D2, 36 km southeast of Compiègne and 255 km from Calais

The beautiful Forêt des Retz makes a thick, tangled mass of deciduous foliage, cut across by avenues along which you can walk, cycle or even (in some cases) drive under the leafy branches. Standing within the margins of this woodland, the little village of Longpont is in every way satisfying. Not only the setting, but its cottages of fine stone, its gardens, its cobbled main street, its spacious village green spread out in front of a majestic ruined abbey, are all wonderfully picturesque.

The skeletal remains of the graceful fourteenth-century Gothic abbey rise high, flying buttresses supporting a façade of golden stone in which a huge empty circle is all that remains of a rose window. Pass within, to find walls and pillars, overgrown with greenery, which date back to the earlier origins of the abbey. St Bernard founded it for the Cistercians in the twelfth century, and in 1227 it was reconsecrated in the presence of Louis IX. At the Revolution the buildings were seized and sold, to be dismantled for their stone, but in 1813 the abbey was purchased by the noble Montesquiou family – who still own it.

Handsome old stone houses surround the grass and gravel village green, Place de l'Abbaye. From the square a gateway leads into a private park bordered on one side by an eighteenth-century mansion in the village's honey-coloured stone: this is the existing abbey.

The cobbled village street passing under Les Tourelles

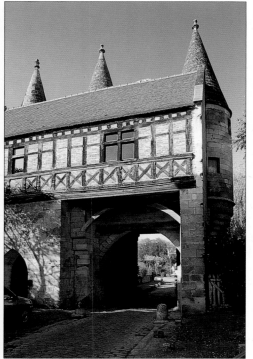

Leading away from the abbey square, yet more attractive houses in the same pale stone line the delightful Rue des Tourelles. Among them, the creeper-clad Hôtel de l'Abbaye has a dozen modest rooms and good, inexpensive menus. A superb gateway, covered with a brick and timber dwelling (occupied) and fortified by four round towers with pointed stone turrets, spans the street. Called Les Tourelles, this once formed part of fourteenth-century ramparts enclosing Longpont. Rue des Tourelles continues just a little further, to rejoin D2, the quiet through-road which skirts the village.

Abbey open April–Oct. at weekends for half-hour, guided visits

VILLERS-HÉLON
On D2, 40 km southeast of Compiègne and 259 km from Calais

Just minutes away from Longpont, and in the same peaceful, attractive landscape of fields, pretty little Villers-Hélon receives few visitors. Hardly more than a single impressive street of fine stone cottages, farmhouses and productive smallholdings, it rises up the slope of a hill to its small and ancient Romanesque church.

A square belfry fortified with a single stone turret beside the porch provides the church with simple defenses. Inside (you will have to ask around to find someone with the key), there have been a few later additions, with barrel-vaulted ceiling and Gothic arches dividing the older interior into three naves. In front of the church, the war memorial, in a curve of green beside the through-road, shows that during the Great War many lives were lost here, but in the Second War only two: a pattern often repeated throughout the region.

Simple fortifications for the village church

NORMANDY

Normandy's borders reach within just 140 kilometres of the Channel Tunnel terminal. The history and landscapes of the duchy strike a satisfying chord of resonance for the British. Its high, wide northern fields seem close to the sky. Beneath those green fields is solid chalk, which opens to the sea in gleaming white cliffs. Along the coast are atmospheric harbours with trawlers at busy working quaysides, and a string of once-stylish resort towns. The inland countryside is profoundly rustic, in places dreamily picturesque.

The best of it lies a little further south. The meandering River Seine, edged with castles, monasteries and white cliffs, twists and turns through a glorious forest landscape. Across the Seine, the Pays d'Auge is reached. With its thatched cottages and orchards, this seems the perfect image of rustic peace. Quiet lanes run between the fruit trees, heavy with pale blossom in spring. Timbered farmhouses have lilies growing along the ridge of thatch, and flower boxes at the windows.

From here came our forebear the Conqueror and his people, joining the duchy to his new kingdom. When William set sail to enforce his claim to the crown of England in 1066, the Normans had only been settled in Normandy for 150 years. His great-grandparents were Vikings – Norsemen, hence the name of Normandy. In the ninth century,

Viking raiders had harried this coast, penetrating its rivers to loot and plunder the rich monasteries, especially along the Seine. In the tenth century, the Vikings had a change of heart, and in the year 911 their far-sighted overlord, Rollo, signed a pact with the Frankish king, Charles the Simple, who promised them a huge duchy of their own if the Vikings would live in peace with their neighbours.

At first it went well. The Normans, as the Vikings settlers became known, traded and farmed and repaired the damage they had done. But before long their roving nature came to the fore, and they tried to expand their territories in every direction. The French king wanted to quell the Norman duchy, but found it impossible to conquer. Then the crown of England came to William, though the Saxons disputed the inheritance. A century more, and the culture and architecture of the Normans was being carried to all their territories, which by then stretched from England and Ireland all the way to Jerusalem. Eventually it went far beyond – there's a Little Dieppe on the coast of Guinea, founded in 1364; a party of Protestant seamen from Le Havre established a colony on the coast of Brazil in 1555; and in 1682, Cavalier de la Salle, with a Norman crew, sailed from Rouen across the Atlantic, through the St Lawrence to the Great Lakes and down the

Mississippi, eventually claiming Louisiana for France. Yet the heartland of the Normans remained the River Seine.

For all that, it is an entirely different image that the river most vividly evokes in modern minds. Perhaps it's pure coincidence that Claude Monet chose to live at Giverny, on Rollo's border at the confluence of the Epte and the Seine; and that he came from Le Havre at the end of the river. But thanks to him the Seine, today, begins and ends with the Impressionists. Along its length from Giverny to the sea, the air and light they longed to capture on canvas dominate all else. Working out-of-doors, with new types of paints which could be used quickly, the artists

Apple harvesting in Normandy

fought to capture a sense of being in the real world, in the open, and of the fleeting quality of images, of the impressions made by light on objects, on space, on the emotions.

Between England and Normandy there always remained something of a two-way traffic. Along the Norman coast English ships came and went during the Hundred Years War, while in the nineteenth century, the Impressionists journeyed across the Channel to London and the Thames. And in this century the beaches of lower Normandy saw another great return, in the mightiest seaborne invasion ever launched, the Allied D-Day landings that were to help end the Second World War.

Maybe the close historical links partly explain why the British are so very fond of the countryside and the architecture of Normandy. The food, too, appeals to our palates. Normandy's cuisine is rich, creamy and yet delicate. Flowering orchards, in which cows idly graze, produce the best of thick, tangy *crème fraîche*, butter, cheeses and, of course, apples. The Pays d'Auge has created some great cheeses. Camembert, Pont l'Évêque and Livarot, for example, all come from here. North of the Seine, they make milder, white, creamy cheeses, like Petit-Suisse, Brillat-Savarin and the more distinguished Neufchâtel. In village markets, many other farm cheeses can be found.

All those apples are mostly for drinking, not eating. Calvados, Normandy's apple brandy, is a fragrant, elegant liquid fire which perfectly concludes a good meal. To start, you could try sparkling pommeau (blended cider and calvados) as an aperitif. Although white wines from the Loire are more popular nowadays, the proper, traditional drink to accompany Normandy dishes is not wine but dry cider, another local speciality.

The fishing towns land vast catches every day. Sole (*sole*), brill (*barbue*) and mackerel (*maquereau*) feature on all the best menus of Normandy. The harbour of Dieppe has given its name to several Normandy favourites, such as *marmite dieppoise*, a herb-flavoured stew of fish and shellfish, and *sole à la dieppoise*, which has the fish cooked in cider (or, less correctly, wine) with shallots, and the sauce thickened with cream and butter. Generous helpings of cream are used in Normandy's sweet and savoury dishes and in rich sauces, especially the ubiquitous *sauce normande* which mixes cream and cider and comes with sea-fresh fish and shellfish. For meatier tastes, Normans also love strongly flavoured tripe, sausages and *pâtés*.

Not for nothing does the custom survive of the *trou normand* – a short break taken in the midst of a huge meal, during which a leisurely glass of calvados is enjoyed. Normans claim that this aids digestion! Rather, it aids conversation, good humour, pleasure and appetite.

As well as scores of delightful villages, Normandy has historic towns and cities which should not be missed. Most are scattered on or near the banks and estuary of the Seine, that immense water highway which for centuries provided the only easy route to the interior. The river loops sharply through Normandy's vivacious capital, Rouen.

A large, industrial city, yet at its heart Rouen remains one of the most attractive towns in northern France. There are streets upon streets of exquisite old houses and shops, of timber or stone, and several really exceptional buildings. The ancient centre lies on the Seine's north bank. Cobbled streets and lanes wander among superb medieval architecture, including a dozen lace-delicate flamboyant Gothic churches, and hundreds of delightful old stone or half-timbered buildings skewwhiff with age.

Above all, the cathedral – painted twenty times (at different hours of the day) by Monet – is an exuberant Gothic fantasy, the focal point of the city. From the cathedral, the old quarter's narrow shopping street, Rue du Gros-Horloge, straddled by the much-photographed gilded medieval clocktower, runs into Place du Vieux Marché, the market square where Jeanne d'Arc (of whom Rouen makes much) was burnt alive in 1431.

Some of the duchy's best eating places are around the square. One of them, Betrand Warin's restaurant, with its handsome courtyard, is among Normandy's top names. There's a tremendous amount to see and do in the city, apart from walking, shopping, and eating out. At least half-a-dozen museums deserve a visit. The city's Fine Arts Museum has a string of rooms devoted to Impressionists and their successors. Views of the Seine appear and reappear, by Monet, Boudin, Sisley and others.

The coastal towns, too, with their lively, seafaring past, include some of special charm. Dieppe, though a large and busy town, with a long history as a tourist resort (it has several nightclubs and a casino), has an attractive, hard-working harbour district. This is no mere tourist sight: Dieppe's fishing fleet is one of the most important in France. Its huge daily street market, too, brings together produce from the whole Caux region, and is crowded with French shoppers.

Although Dieppe has a sandy beach, with a row of sedate hotels set back on a clifftop with fine sea views, the old, atmospheric centre of town is its deep natural harbour. Here trawlers park while their haul is bought and sold on the quayside. Over half the *coquilles St Jacques* (scallops) eaten in France come from here. Not surprisingly, the town has several excellent fish restaurants.

The pedestrianized main street, Grande Rue, runs to busy Place du Puit Salé, where the dingy eighteenth-century inn Les Tribunaux was the place Oscar Wilde favoured for a drink in his sad exile during the 1890s. Aubrey Beardsley would have been seen here at the same time.

Only a decade before, the Tribunaux was the meeting point for young Impressionists, including many destined to become world-famous – Renoir, Monet, Pissarro, Sickert and Whistler. Some of their works can be seen in the town's museum, which is housed in a fifteenth-century clifftop château.

Southward, other dignified old resort towns, St-Valéry, Fécamp, Etretat, shelter at the foot of dramatic white cliffs. Across the Seine estuary, Honfleur is a fishing town with an impressive old harbour, Le Vieux Bassin. Trawlers still work here, their fish and shellfish being landed almost straight into the kitchens of popular quayside restaurants. Tall, narrow buildings, slate covered, enclose the dock. Round the corner in cobbled Place Ste-Cathérine, the lovely wooden church was built by shipwrights, not masons.

Here too, the early Impressionists came to paint, especially Monet and Boudin (whose father was an Honfleur fisherman). It seems that artists still find the place appealing, and there are several art galleries close to the waterfront. Further down the coast, some of the great *fin-de-siècle* beach resorts, especially Deauville, cling to memories of their former grandeur. They are just minutes away from the exquisite villages of the Pays d'Auge.

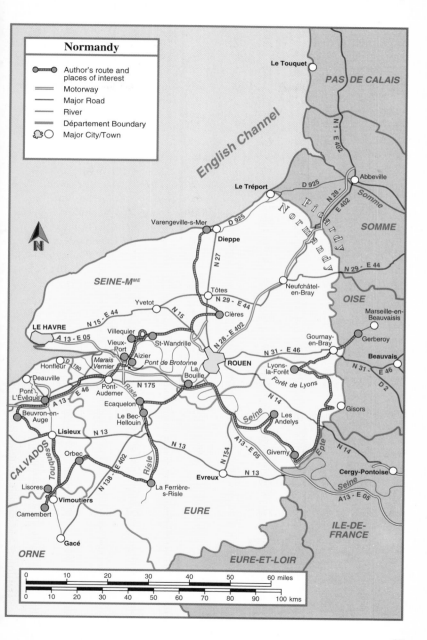

Normandy

- Author's route and places of interest
- Motorway
- Major Road
- River
- Département Boundary
- Major City/Town

Le Touquet

PAS DE CALAIS

English Channel

Abbeville

Le Tréport

D 925

Somme

N 1 - E 402

N 28 -

E 402

Varengeville-s-Mer D 925

SOMME

Picardy

Normandy

Dieppe

N 27

Neufchâtel-en-Bray

N 29 - E 44

OISE

SEINE-MME

Tôtes

N 29 - E 44

Yvetot

N 15

Clères

Marseille-en-Beauvaisis

LE HAVRE

N 15 - E 44

A 13 - E 05

Villequier

Vieux-Port

St-Wandrille

Aizier

Pont de Brotonne

N 28 - E 402

ROUEN

Gournay-en-Bray

N 31 - E 46

Gerberoy

Beauvais

N 31 -

E 46

Honfleur

D 180

Marais Vernier

La Bouille

Lyons-la-Forêt

D 2

Deauville

Pont-L'Evêque

A 13

E 46

Pont-Audemer

N 175

Forêt de Lyons

Beuvron-en-Auge

Ecaquelon

Risle

Seine

Les Andelys

Gisors

Lisieux

N 13

Le Bec-Hellouin

N 13

N 154

A 13 - E 05

Giverny

Epte

N 14

Cergy-Pontoise

Orbec

N 13

Evreux

N 13

Seine

Touques

N 138 - E 402

Risle

La Ferrière-s-Risle

A13 - E 05

Lisores

CALVADOS

Vimoutiers

EURE

ILE-DE-FRANCE

Camembert

Gacé

ORNE

EURE-ET-LOIR

| 0 | 10 | 20 | 30 | 40 | 50 | 60 miles |

| 0 | 10 | 20 | 30 | 40 | 50 | 60 | 70 | 80 | 90 | 100 kms |

GERBEROY
Beside junction of D930 and D133, 20 km northwest of Beauvais and 203 km from Calais

On the border of Picardy and Normandy (lying on the Picardy side), little Gerberoy has perfect, chocolate-box charm. A narrow, winding main street, edged with cobbled pavements, slopes gently into the village, passing through the gateways of old brick ramparts. To either side, greenery and flowers drape delightful brick and timber cottages. Dormer windows peep through the roofs. Hydrangeas heavy with huge blooms burst forth along the foot of houses. Climbing roses and leafy creepers cling to walls. One house, unoccupied for a while, has been buried entirely in foliage like a shaggy dog, while others have a pristine tidiness. There's a tiny cobbled square to one side.

At the foot of the village, the little street reaches a thrillingly pretty *place* like a small village green, with patches of lawn, hedges, flower beds, an old well and three great chestnuts with shading boughs. Here stands a covered market of brick and timber. A side road, all cobbled, passes behind the market and climbs to meet a couple of other idyllic, flowery back lanes. A corner cottage, the white and

Greenery and flowers and cobbled lanes

blue Maison Bleue, is quite exquisite.

The lanes rise to another fortified brick gateway, partly ruined but clearly once substantial. Pass through to reach Gerberoy's church, up on little ridge. A sign urges visitors to 'Please close the door because of the swallows'. Inside, most of the ceiling is wooden, barrel-vaulted, and there are attractively carved wooden choir stalls and good statuary. In front of the building, a miniature terrace gives a view across the steep, red-tiled roofs and the gardens into the rolling countryside of fields and copses.

Once, Gerberoy was an important border fortress held by Normandy. Indeed, in 1079 the Duke of Normandy, William the Conqueror himself, was injured here – by his son Robert. Even by the end of the Middle Ages it had already begun to decline into insignificance. But in the nineteenth-century it was taken up by the painter Henri le Sidanier, together with a number of other artists and writers, who kept it alive and made the village aware of its beauty. The place indeed could hardly be more pleasing if it had been created simply as a work of art.

Yet only a few visitors come here. Parked cars would look quite out of place – so do please park in the gravelled area outside the lower gate, Porte Guillaume le Conquérant. The lane heading north from the village continues the picture-book theme, with neatly clipped and shaped hedges leading down to a hamlet around a riverside manor house.

LYONS-LA-FORÊT
On D6, D2, and D32, 25 km east of Rouen and 224 km from Calais

The 10,700 hectares of the Forêt de Lyons which lies just east of Rouen and just north of the river Seine are not unbroken woodland, but a patchwork of extensive beechwoods and sunlit cornfields, scattered with pleasant, rural villages. At its heart, Lyons-la-Forêt is a wonderfully satisfying village. From here, a dozen lovely walks or drives can be started, though it's a delight, too, to remain in Lyons, strolling or sitting at a café table in the market square at its heart.

The square, Place Benserade, forms a magnificent ensemble of fine old houses, almost all heavily timbered. A splendid wooden *halles*, or covered market, long and

The picturesque market square at Lyons-la-Forêt

narrow, takes up most of the square. Fixed to one end of it, the original handwritten sign requests the public to refrain from tying their horses to the posts. Markets still take place here every Saturday and Sunday morning.

Next to the covered market, café tables are arranged invitingly around a fountain. A good *pâtissier-chocolatier* (with the not very local name of C. Przygoda) is well placed to provide a little something. Just off the square, Hôtel Licorne has been an *auberge* since 1610, and is today a three-star Château-Indépendant hotel and restaurant. There's another unusual hotel, Domaine St Paul, amid quiet fields just outside the village on the D921, combining moderate prices, reasonable accommodation, extensive grounds and good leisure facilities.

Despite its appeal, Lyons has not been taken over by tourists and is very much a living village, bustling with little shops.

From the market place, stroll along the curve of Rue de l'Hôtel de Ville, passing the local *mairie* (town hall) and *syndicat d'initiative* (information office). Wooded, green slopes rise up ahead. The road descends to another, separate part of Lyons, equally picturesque and running alongside a stream. It's quite a walk along here and across the stream to reach the village church. This attractive stone building, originally twelfth century, but much changed in the fifteenth, contains excellent timberwork and impressive wooden statues. They provide beautiful testimony to the skill and piety of the local people who for centuries derived their livelihoods entirely from the forest and its timber.

GIVERNY
On D313, 64 km southeast of Rouen and 282 km from Calais

Its name is synonymous all over the world with the house and the glorious gardens created by one man: Claude Monet, the founder of Impressionism. He was enthralled, like most early Impressionists, by the pearly, luminous air over the Seine valley, especially near its estuary. Indeed, his first paintings were around Honfleur and Le Havre. In 1833, having already established himself as a pioneer artist, he came to live at Giverny, a village on the very frontier of Normandy, overlooking the confluence of the Seine and the Epte.

Monet's house at Giverny ...

In the year 911, Rollo the Viking and Charles the Simple – meeting beside its waters – agreed that the Epte would be the border of the Norsemen's new duchy. Hardly had they

agreed to live in peace within these limits than the Dukes of Normandy became a threat to all their neighbours and to the French monarchy, and the forces of the king began their constant struggle to contain and reconquer the duchy.

Giverny itself recalls little of this. The quiet, unpretentious village consists of little more than a single long lane of houses along a gentle hillside. A small main road, D5, passes below the village. It is right at the village end, as the street slopes down to join D5, that Monet's house can be found. It is a national monument, French flags fly above the front door, and a large car park in front gives warning of how many people come here at the height of the season.

The house gives a fascinating glimpse into life in the late nineteenth century. A wooden box on the wall is marked *œufs frais* (fresh eggs). The kitchen, its walls entirely covered with blue tiles, is neat, spacious and well ordered. In the dining room is a photograph of Monet in that very room. Upstairs, the artist's large bedroom has bare boards, simple, wooden furniture and a picture of his mother above the bed. The mattress is terribly lumpy!

None of Monet's paintings can be found here – they are on view only in the world's top galleries and collections. Instead, the walls are richly decorated, as they were during

... and his famous water garden

the artist's lifetime, with oriental pictures.

Just one of Monet's works can be seen – the garden. This is a masterpiece, glorious in any season. Wide beds of tall flowers border square areas of lawn and trees. The garden extends to the other side of the main road, an underpass joing the two sections.

Beyond the main road the watergardens are to be found: lily ponds circled by footpaths among the trees and crossed by little wooden bridges. After moving to this house, Monet became preoccupied with these gardens and painted them again and again, the simple arched bridge among the water lilies becoming one of his most recognized images.

Monet's house and garden open April–Oct., a.m. and p.m. Closed Mon. and at Easter

---

PETIT ANDELY
On D313 40 km east of Rouen and 250 km from Calais

Marked on the map as Les Andelys, the *commune* is made up of Grand Andely and its prettier little riverside neighbour, Petit Andely. The treasure of the smaller – and older – village is its waterfront, where a broad greensward like a fragment of meadow extends along the bank of the Seine. The river runs behind the houses and shops of Petit Andelys' short main street.

Sit by the water here on a fine day, savouring the view northward along the high, chalk escarpments which follow a great bend in the river, made especially lovely at this point by a string of little islands. Turn the other way and just south of the village rises Richard the Lionheart's superb white fortress, Château Gaillard, impressive on its hilltop.

The castle's name reflects its character. *Gaillard* means bold, brave, with a touch of swagger and panache. Striking in both position and appearance, the château took less than a year to build (a phenomenal achievement – medieval fortresses usually took many years or even decades), and dared to proclaim to the forces of the Kingdom of France that beyond this point the Duchy of Normandy could not be conquered. And nor could it – within Richard's lifetime. Yet as soon as he died and the throne of England and

The Villages of Northern France

The white stone ruins of Château Gaillard gaze across Petit Andely to the Seine's chalk cliffs beyond

Normandy passed to King John, the French took Château Gaillard without delay and travelled swiftly downstream to conquer Rouen. The château amply rewards a visit, whether you make the steep walk up from the village or take the longer route by car.

In other ways, too, Petit Andely made a barrier. It was here that a chain hung right across the Seine, preventing shipping from passing until a toll had been paid. So much money was generated that it became known as the *chaine d'or*, the golden chain. The tollhouse on the little quay has now become the enticing Hôtel de la Chaine d'Or. Its prestigious dining room looks out directly on to the waters of the Seine.

The front of the hotel is a courtyard opening on to Petit Andely's picturesque little street. The handsome old Gothic church of St Sauveur stands in the square opposite.

Château Gaillard open mid-March–mid-Nov., a.m. and p.m. Closed Tue., Wed. a.m.

LA BOUILLE
On D64, 20 km southwest of Rouen and 220 km from Calais

Claude Monet, living a few miles upstream, often travelled to Rouen and beyond to this hamlet beside the Seine. Unfortunately, nowadays a lot of other people love it as much as he did. The village, squeezed between the river bank and a steep, high cliff, has given up the battle against tourists and now seems to have almost as many hotels and restaurants as houses. Fortunately the general standard is good and it remains a pleasure to sit and dine with a river view, then digest gently with a stroll at the waterside.

On a quiet day, midweek, early or late in the year, the village and the setting, with its toes and fingertips touching the broad river as it sweeps round a wide bend, are sheer delight. A tiny *bac* (car ferry) chugs across to and from its little platform here.

The centre of the riverside village

At the top of the cliff, Robert le Diable's Castle also draws crowds. This splendid fortress loses a little by being right beside the *autoroute*. It offers a Viking Museum, refreshments and a superb view of the Seine. No one knows, any more, who Robert le Diable actually was, if indeed he ever existed, though the name may have been given to some illegitimate scion of an early Duke of Normandy. Presumably, pretty La Bouille and its river crossing belonged to him.

Robert le Diable's Castle open daily March–Nov.

ECAQUELON
On D576 (off D124), 26 km southwest of Rouen and 244 km from Calais

Hidden in glorious woods at the end of a tangle of lanes, Ecaquelon has a secretive air. The woodland, a pleasing mixture of beech and fir trees, penetrated by footpaths, embraces the little village and its farms. Old timbered houses, placed at all angles to one another, stand at intervals along the winding, hilly lanes.

There is little to find at the centre. The stone and brick church, on a high ledge of land, occupies the focal point. To judge from its fine tower with a turret on one corner, the size of the building and the size of the graveyard, Ecaquelon was once bigger than today. Inside the church, too, fine wooden carvings dating from the sixteenth century hint at a greater importance in those days. Today it is barely more than a rustic hamlet among the trees. Only a ruler-straight railway line passing through contests the satisfying disorder of the village.

LE BEC-HELLOUIN
On D39 (off D130), 37 km southwest of Rouen and 255 km from Calais

The Risle cuts a wide corridor of soft greenery across that part of Normandy, high, flat, open and fertile, which lies just south of the Seine. On the bank of a tributary of the Risle, the tiny River Bec, a rich nobleman called Herluin (or Hellouin) came to reside in solitude and prayer in the year 1034. Determined to abandon luxury and self-indulgence, the story goes that his first move was to exchange his fine charger for a humble donkey. This simple renunciation had so strong an appeal that just seven years later a community of more than thirty monks – many from distinguished or noble families – had gathered around Herluin.

At that stage the riverside community moved a little upstream, and settled on the site of the present village. In the same year, another devout young man, Lanfranc, already a renowned religious scholar, joined the group. He rose to become abbot, and made the Bec community an influential intellectual centre. Several of its novices graduated to become important ecclesiatical figures, even popes.

Lanfranc moved on to become Archbishop of Canterbury (1070–1081), and was succeeded at Bec by another leading theologian of the day, Anselm of Aosta. He, too, later became Archbishop of Canterbury (1093–1109). After St Anselm, Theobald became the third son of the abbey of Bec-Hellouin to become Archbishop of Canterbury (1138–1161). Three more became Bishop of Rochester and several went to other English religious houses. From Bec came abbots of Westminster, Ely, Colchester, Battle, Chester and Bury St Edmunds.

In subsequent centuries, the abbey passed into the possession of private families, then was abandoned, but in the seventeenth century revived only to be largely ruined again and the monks dispersed at the French Revolution. However, in 1948 the grounds and buildings again came back to the Benedictines who have taken up residence once more and transformed the seventeenth-century refectory into a church. The sarcophagus of Herluin still lies here.

Le Bec-Hellouin: terraces of half-timbered houses

The Villages of Northern France

Enter the abbey grounds through the sturdy stone gateway. Inside, fine old trees shade the lawns of a spacious walled park, peaceful and calm. One may walk freely in the grounds, while the abbey is open only for guided visits. Of the original buildings, the fifteenth-century St Nicholas' Tower and a great wall of the cloister with a fourteenth-century Gothic doorway remain: they alone give some idea of the size and importance of the original abbey beside the Bec. The massive square tower rises like a piece of fretwork, the sky luminous through the bare openings which once were windows. On the its wall a plaque, put in place by the English in 1930, recalls the 'close rapport which united the former abbey of Bec-Hellouin with the Church of England in the eleventh and twelfth centuries'.

Outside the abbey grounds, the village of Le Bec-Hellouin is thoroughly picturesque, a pleasing shape, a marvellous collection of old half-timbered houses in attractive terraces. The focal point is the village green, a big triangle of grass, where mature trees – willow, plane, birch and fir – stand broad and tall. Alongside the green, one row of especially fine timbered houses makes a superb sight, all different heights, roofs all different ages. The best looking of them, with a lower storey of stone blocks, is the

A rustic setting for Le Bec-Hellouin's ancient abbey

appealing hotel-restaurant Auberge de l'Abbaye. A sign on the door offers *cidre bouché*, *tarte à la crême* and other Normandy specialities.

Of course, such a place as this does attract tourists in season, and around the village several other restaurants can be found. As an additional entertainment for visitors, away from the village centre, there's even a car museum with vehicles dating from the 1920s and all in working order. Yet in spring and autumn Le Bec-Hellouin remains quiet and deserted. The Bec is a delightful stream. Woods and little fields climb uphill away to either side.

Abbey open daily excluding Tue. for guided tours a.m. and p.m.; Sun. and fêtes p.m. only. Car museum open daily a.m. and p.m., closed Wed. and Thur. in winter

LA FERRIÈRE-SUR-RISLE
On D140, 65 km south of Rouen and 283 km from Calais

La Ferrière on the right bank, with smaller Ajou on the left, make a single, quiet, attractive village of old houses beside the delightful River Risle. Some dwellings are of stone, some of brick in different shades giving a patterned, almost chequered appearance, but most are half-timbered wattle and daub, with many crisscrossed, zig-zagging timbers. The houses form two streets facing each other across a broad market square.

A fourteenth-century timber *halles*, or covered marketplace, stands at the centre of the square. Just beyond it, the two streets come together beside one especially fine old house with an arcaded pavement. Opposite, the Hôtel du Croissant has good set menus.

At the other end of the village, the streets meet again at the unusual early Gothic thirteenth-century church of St Georges, an official *monument historique*. Inside it's an odd shape, with elaborate altars and statuary dominated by a Louis XIV high altar. An extremely ornate, gilded, baroque altarpiece of oak, dating from the sixteenth century, has a *Descent from the Cross* believed (by experts at the Louvre) to be the work of a student or assistant of Leonardo da Vinci. The barrel-vaulted roof is supported by crossbeams bearing

Stone, brick and timber at La Ferrière-sur-Risle

crests. There's a statue of the parish saint, Saint George the dragonslayer, with a small sign beneath giving the information that George was decapitated in the year 303 and can be invoked against eczema!

Outside the church, Place de la Mairie is a pleasant area – more an open space than a square – with greenery, trees and flower beds. A third street leads from the church to the river where trees overhang the water and gardens grow along the bank. On the other side, the hamlet of Ajou has the same pleasing mix of half-timbered and patterned brick houses. Beyond, sheep graze in meadows, and wooded slopes rise from the Risle.

ORBEC
On D4 and D519, 82 km southwest of Rouen and 300 km from Calais

Orbec lies on the eastern edge of the Pays d'Auge, which extends from here some 40 kilometres west. It's one of the most appealing and attractive areas in northern France, a

lush and rustic land of winding lanes, small hills and
wooded valleys. The countryside seems all on a small,
intimate scale. Its little orchards produce famous apples
from which the equally famous calvados and cider are
made, its contented cows produce milk from which famous
cream and cheeses are made. The traditional Pays d'Auge
architecture of heavily timbered houses under thickly
thatched roofs satisfies the eye and the soul. A feature of the
local style is the many exposed, angled beams, often
decoratively crisscrossed. Between the great timbers may be
slender bricks or wattle and daub, and along the crest of the
thatch there's frequently a pretty row of lilies growing. A
curious extension of the roof, or an overhanging gable,
provides some shelter for firewood piled against the outer
wall. Although the farmhouses and cottages of the region
are exquisite, another distinctive feature of the Pays d'Auge
is its imposing manor houses – looking something between a
farmhouse and a château.

A small and lively country town, Orbec runs mainly
along a single, bustling street, Rue Grande. On both sides,
and in the few narrow sidestreets, stand fine old houses of
patterned brickwork and timber. Miniscule alleys, called
venelles (the same word used in some parts of the north of

*Orbec stands on
the edge of the
Pays d'Auge*

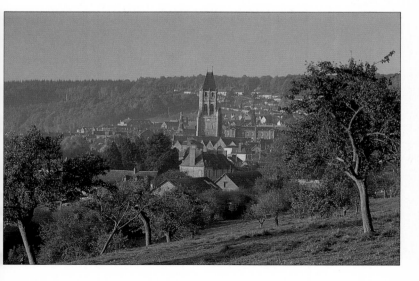

England), thread between buildings. Many houses reveal, behind gateways or open doors, lovely cobbled courtyards, almost like small public squares, and indeed some are now enclosed by dwellings.

Number 54 Rue Grande, for example, has a delightful courtyard with other houses inside. Number 75 has superb medieval brick and timber. Number 107 is a magnificent medieval corner house. You'll see a sign to the *musée*, a municipal museum inside one of the grandest houses, the sixteenth-century Vieux Manoir. It houses collections of local everyday objects, with archaeological and historical displays.

Half way along the main street, the charmless brick façade of the battered church of the *hôtel-Dieu* (or hospice) stands out; this landmark is an ancient one, the tower dating from the thirteenth century. At the end of Rue Grande looms the bulk of a stocky church in stone, its big square tower topped by an incongruous touch of Renaissance frivolity.

An example of Orbec's fine brickwork and timberwork

Among the greatest delights of the Auge countryside are its lovely little rivers, flowing in their quiet green valleys. Orbec stands beside one of the most appealing of them, the Orbiquet. Just 5 kilometres away from town is the river's picturesque spring.

To find it (*La Source de l'Orbiquet*), take D130A towards neighbouring La Folletière-Abenon.

Museum open daily p.m. in July and Aug.; rest of year weekend p.m. only; closed Tue.

LISORES

On D268, 104 km southwest of Rouen and 322 km from Calais

Head up a tiny country lane through a typically rustic Auge terrain of little hills and hedgerows, trickling streams and grazing cows, apple orchards carpeted with rich grass, the trees heavily laden with blossom in spring and fruit in autumn. At last the tall, slender, red-brick church spire of Lisores comes into view, and you arrive at this modest hamlet of farmhouses and gardens. Though small, it has a *mairie*: a sweet little corner house of brick on the edge of the village.

The family of artist Fernand Léger (1881–1955) owned Bougonnière Farm, in the hills beside the village. He often came here to relax, think and paint. One of the farm's barns, and an adjoining garden, have become the Musée Fernand Léger, a fine memorial created by his wife Nadia in a marvellous setting. To find it, go only about 500 metres past the *mairie* down a lane (numbered C1), signposted

The rustic hamlet of Lisores

St-Foy-de-Montgommery. The museum displays interesting models of stained glass, mosaics, paintings, statues and tapestries based on, or copied from, Léger though there are also a few original examples of his own work. Photographs show him at work in the barn, which he used as a studio.

Fernand Léger Museum open daily April–Oct., a.m. and p.m.; Nov.–March, a.m. and p.m. on weekends and fêtes only

CAMEMBERT
Off D246, 108 km southwest of Rouen and 326 km from Calais

Today the busy country town of Vimoutiers considers itself the capital of Camembert, and certainly the milk for this most successful of Normandy cheeses is produced in abundance by the cows in the surrounding meadows. The sharp aroma of cheese rises from manufacturing dairies on the outskirts, and there's a statue in town of the 'inventor' of Camembert cheese, Marie Harel.

Madame Harel, well-to-do farmer's wife, so improved the traditional, soft, creamy but tangy local cheese that her version supplanted all rivals and became established as the only true Camembert. One legend is that she was given the recipe by a priest whom she hid during the French Revolution. Another is that the success of her cheese followed from her husband handing a box of it to Napoleon when the Emperor happened to be visiting the region. Perhaps both are true.

Just 5 kilometres away from Vimoutiers is the village of Camembert itself, a simple hamlet on a hill. At the foot of the hill, beside the Viette stream, stands another monument to Marie Harel: *'Née Marie Fontaine, 1761–1812, qui inventa le camembert.'* This memorial was erected by an American doctor who considered Camembert the cure for his stomach pains! And at the top of the hill, above the rest of the village, can be seen the fine timbered farmhouse where Madame Harel once lived. The setting is marvellous, rich Pays d'Auge scenery of lush, green meadows, copses and spinneys, and orchards of apple and pear growing on a dense mat of grass.

The tiny village climbs up from the Viette, on the slope

Camembert's museum resembles an opened cheesebox

of a hill. The Norman tower of a fourteenth-century church rises over the wattle and daub farmhouses with their massive timbers. The *mairie*, decked out with flags, stands beside the Maison du Camembert, a curiously designed building made to resemble an opened circular Camembert cheesebox. Inside, you can buy the cheese, and learn about it from displays and a film.

All around the village farms offer their own traditional Camembert made on the premises. The best are excellent, incomparably better than the usual factory-made cheese. Two farms in particular, Herronière and Tourdouet, both on the main trunk road (D916) above the village, remain loyal to the Marie Harel recipe and method, making their cheese with fresh milk straight from the cow.

Maison du Camembert open weekdays a.m. and p.m.

The Villages of Northern France

BEUVRON-EN-AUGE
On D49, 108 km west of Rouen and 326 km from Calais

Travel from the cheese and calvados country around Vimoutiers, along the pastoral valley of the Touques (the road is D64). To either side, superb old manor houses, heavy with timbers, sometimes moated, stand among their farms. Pause to admire the best of them at Chiffretot, near les Moutiers-Hubert; at Bellou, with its village; at Fervaques, on the very bank of the river; and, especially impressive, at St Germaine-de-Livet, also on the riverside. The Touques then meets the Orbiquet in the streets of Lisieux, after which the Touques valley continues wider, flowing pleasantly between orchards, to the Channel.

From Lisieux, instead of following the Touques, a lovely rural ride can be made along narrow lanes wandering through one of the prettiest corners of the Pays d'Auge: travel first to the old abbey of Le Val Richer, some 6 kilometres west of the town; then through Montreuil-en-Auge; past the church, with its panoramic view, at Clermont-en-Auge; to reach Beuvron-en-Auge.

In the village centre   Beuvron is the very model of the picturesque Pays

d'Auge village, all of ancient timbered houses, flower-filled window boxes and cobbled pavements. At its centre, in Place du Village, a crooked old covered marketplace heaps on the charm, and on a corner of the market square there's an excellent, long-established restaurant, Le Pavé d'Auge, its façade a herringbone zigzag of weathered beams.

At the end of the village street, Beuvron's manor house completes the scene, a masterpiece of rustic elegance, a mass of carved timbers. The lords of the manor have gone but theirs is still the finest house of all in this picturebook setting.

VIEUX-PORT
On D65, 20 km southwest from Brotonne Bridge and 255 km from Calais

From the villages of the Pays d'Auge, it's a short drive through the cheese towns of Pont l'Évêque and Pont Audemer to the rather different scenery and atmosphere of the lower Seine Valley.

In the past, the meandering Seine had a more capricious nature than today, with its floods, tidal bore and even changes in its course. Its estuary lengthened, widened and became banked with broad flats of alluvial sand and soil. Close to its mouth, a great loop of river disappeared, leaving an extensive marshland: the Marais Vernier. This marsh has been 'reclaimed' – drained and cultivated – and today lies like a flat-bottomed basin full of greenery. A good view of the Marais (and of the soaring Tancarville Bridge beyond) can be enjoyed from the slope just below Ste-Opportune-la-Mare (follow the signs to the *Réserve de Faune de la Grand' Mare* and *Panorama de la Grand' Mare*). In the foreground is the Grande Mare lake, now a wildlife preserve.

Only 4 kilometres (on D95) separate Ste-Opportune from an especially lovely stretch of the Seine. As the road reaches the river, it turns to give a broad view of the valley, then descends steeply through woods, orchards and little fields into the peaceful, pretty village of Vieux-Port, which lies in a hollow at the edge of the water.

The place is a cornucopia of gardens. Most of the houses are gorgeous examples of the thatched, half-timbered country style, with a line of lilies growing in the crest of the

thatch, reminiscent of the Pays d'Auge. The village touches
the river at an open space behind the parish church, giving
a fine view across the water.

AIZIER
On D65, 14 km southwest from Brotonne Bridge and 249 km from Calais

A picturesque group of cottages gathered around an old
stone church, on a gentle slope beside a flood meadow of
the lapping Seine, Aizier feels remote and tranquil. The
houses vary in age and style from ancient to modern, from
tiny cottages to mansions, yet all blend happily together.
Around them, well-tended gardens may be devoted to
decorative flowers or become productive miniature
smallholdings. A few of the cottages are astonishingly small:
one behind the church surely contains hardly more than a
single room.

The simple church under its stone roof and handsome
Romanesque square stone tower dates mainly from the
twelfth century. The enclosed graveyard outside once
formed part of the church itself. Beside the churchyard
wall, a curious stone slab with a circular hole in the centre
came from a 3,000-year-old burial mound.

The narrow lane of the D65, sometimes winding crazily
among the trees, leads away from the village, running
beside the beech forests of the Brotonne Regional Park and
close to the curving Seine. Glimpses down into the vast
river valley give a powerful impression of its majestic shape,
space and size. The road passes through a succession of
hamlets and villages of beautifully half-timbered houses,
many under grassy thatched roofs, clustered together in
rolling green pasture, sometimes with a more substantial
dwelling in brick and pale stone. Numerous exquisite little
farms consist of no more than a few tiny fields with hens
and cows, an orchard of just a few trees, and a ramshackle
farmhouse of red-painted timbers and pale walls. Many of
the buildings, especially the barns, have the characteristic
overhanging gable of Lower Normandy. Across the river,
the white chalk escarpments of the north bank rise to a
crest of woodland.

In the time when people travelled on water rather than

land, the Seine was a great highway, navigable from the sea to the capital. Even modern ships reach inland to the docks at Rouen. When roads began to replace rivers, though, the Seine became an immense barrier to travel and trade. It could only be crossed on the tiny ferries which still operate at dozens of places. For twentieth-century travellers, the bridge at Tancarville, near the estuary, was a vital breakthrough. When it opened in 1959, it was the river's only road crossing between Rouen and Le Havre. Not until 1977 was another bridge constructed – the Pont de Brotonne. Now a third bridge, the Pont de Normandie can take traffic across the wide estuary.

D65 arrives at the very foot of the elegant Pont de Brotonne. On its high arc over the water, you seem almost to take flight into the luminescent Seine valley skies.

VILLEQUIER
On D81, 40 km west of Rouen and 250 km from Calais

The Brotonne bridge soars past the north bank of the Seine: to reach the river, you must return on the minor left turning signposted to Caudebec-en-Caux. This ancient waterside town, once famous for its picturesque streets, was systematically destroyed as an act of vengeance by retreating Germans at the end of the Second World War. Today it has been rebuilt but in modern style. Take the riverside road D81 downstream for 5 kilometres to the village of Villequier.

Spreading itself along the Seine waterfront, Villequier enjoys a calm atmosphere and has almost nothing in the way of shops or commerce. There's a wonderful riverside promenade, and, parallel to it, a single street lined by an assortment of old houses, some brick, some stone, some half-timbered. There is only a vague suggestion of a village centre at the crossroads where little Rue Réné Coty comes down from the church, crosses the main through-road, and continues as Rue Auguste Vacquerie for another few paces to reach the river.

The waterside quay runs the full length of the village, a pleasant kilometre or two with a superb view, strolling between the lapping water and the villagers' back gardens (some large and beautifully tended). Looking ahead, on one side, the Seine valley rises abruptly in chalky escarpments crowned with woods, while across the river the country lies flat under the vast sky. The water, perhaps, is none too clean after its long journey, but the light and air are inspiring. No wonder Impressionists gathered in this area.

Until the flow of the Seine came under more careful control in this century, the riverfront between Villequier and Caudebec used to be witness to a spectacular tidal bore, known as *le mascaret*. At the equinoxes in March and September, when it was especially dramatic, people would gather on the quay to watch the rush of flood water surging upstream.

The largest and most delightful of the waterside gardens lies behind a large house – from the front, it seems to be three knocked into one – which used to be the home of an important local family, the Vacqueries, prosperous from shipbuilding. Charles Vacquerie married Léopoldine Hugo, daughter of the writer Victor Hugo. The Hugo family became close to the Vacqueries and often visited. Six months after their wedding, Charles and Léopoldine came back here to watch the famous flood tide. The water was higher than usual, and more violent. It rose above the river

The family home of the Vacqueries, in-laws of Victor Hugo, has become a museum

embankment and swept along the Villequier promenade like a broom. The newlyweds were both drowned.

The Vacquerie family home has become the Victor Hugo Museum, in which letters, furniture and other possessions recapture something of that tragedy, and of the life of the Vacquerie household in those days. The manuscript of *Les Contemplations*, in which Victor Hugo wrote about his grief, which never healed, is on display.

Return to the small, aisle-less village church, which has a turreted roof, a fine doorway, and inside, a superb timber roof and stained glass. In the tiny cemetery outside are the graves of 'Charles Vacquerie, twenty-six years, and Léopoldine Vacquerie, née Hugo, nineteen years, married 15 February and died 4 September'. Beside them lies Victor Hugo's wife, Adèle, who chose to be buried here near her daughter.

Victor Hugo Museum open daily a.m. and p.m. excluding Tue., Mon. in winter, and some fêtes

---

ST-WANDRILLE
On D33, off D81, 36 km west of Rouen and 246 km from Calais

Return along the river, passing Caudebec, to the lane which leads to the pretty crossroads hamlet of St-Wandrille where timbered houses cluster together at the foot of a delightful, green hill. The ringing bells and white stone of its great, old abbey dominate the village. Only the passage of summer tourists disturbs a historic calm.

A large ornamental nineteenth-century gateway, poised importantly on a corner, appears to be the main entrance to the abbey grounds, but this is rarely used. In fact, the entrance is a fifteenth-century doorway in the wall, which opens into a large cool enclosed courtyard and garden, formal with wide gravel paths and neat hedges. Monks, with cropped hair and long brown robes secured by a lengthy black leather belt, may be seen passing to and fro or perhaps working with clippers and shears to keep the plant beds tidy. Along one side of the courtyard the present-day abbey adjoins the massive ruined walls and Gothic pillars of an earlier cathedral-like building. This was the abbey church, built in the thirteenth and fourteenth centuries, and even what little remains gives an awesome impression of size and dignity.

The Benedictine community of St-Wandrille has been remarkably tenacious. Wandrille himself, called 'God's Athlete' for his exceptional physique, decided, on his wedding day in the year 649, to devote himself instead to the service of God. His bride spent the rest of her life in a convent. Wandrille's monastery was founded here in the valley of the little Fontanelle, just a few hundred metres from the north bank of the Seine. Within two centuries, because of Wandrille and the community he had founded, the Fontanelle became known as the Valley of Saints.

In those days the Seine, lined with commerce and newly established religious houses, was a veritable highway from the Ile de France to the sea. In the ninth and tenth centuries it became a favourite route for Vikings intent on plunder and destruction. The Fontanelle monastery was destroyed. But almost at once the Vikings made their peace with France and were granted the Duchy of Normandy, on condition that the damage done was made good. St-Wandrille's monastery was rebuilt, and the community returned. The Wars of Religion in the sixteenth century

The little fifteenth-century gateway into St-Wandrille's abbey

exacted a severe toll in their turn, and the Revolution brought complete and seemingly final destruction.

Yet less than a century later the abbey of St-Wandrille was once more reborn, and fine new buildings were put up beside the old ruins. A delightful small church – where the Gregorian chant can again be heard during services – is today housed in a 700-year-old barn brought here stone by stone from a village across the Seine. Beside the church, you can see into the abbey's extensive gardens where monks labour to produce all their own food. Beyond rise steep, wooded slopes.

All this countryside comes within the Parc Régional du Brotonne which extends across the Seine. Travel along any of the four roads out of St-Wandrille to pass immediately into a rich, satisfying landscape of woods, pasture and farmland rising away from the river.

Monastery cloisters open daily p.m. for one-hour guided tours; also a.m. on Sun. and fêtes

CLÈRES
On D6 and D155 20 km north of Rouen and 207 km from Calais

The little River Clerette passing through its centre, and a pleasant square with an old wooden covered market, give this large village a degree of low-key charm. By good luck it also happens to be in an untypically picturesque part of Upper Normandy's Caux country, with wooded hills all around. An odd mix of functional, postwar brick with occasional older, more attractive, timbered dwellings lines the few streets, and café tables stand invitingly out of doors. However, Clères does not rely on that to attract visitors.

On a corner just across the road from the covered market, a museum of vehicles (Musée de l'Automobile et Militaire) boasts an astonishing array of early cars, bicycles, fire engines, lorries and miltary vehicles – including an early aeroplane.

At the edge of the village (on the road towards Pavilly) a popular zoo occupies the grounds of a château, originally fourteenth-century but now, extensively renovated, mainly nineteenth-century. Flamingos, peacocks and exotic fowl, kangaroos, antelopes, gibbons and many other creatures wander freely. There's a lake with 120 species of waders and aviaries with over 450 other species of birds.

Children would love Clères. And only a couple of kilometres away, Parc du Bocasse is a children's amusement park with picnic areas.

Vehicle museum open daily all year. Zoo open March–Nov., a.m. and p.m. Parc de Bocasse open daily May–Sept. and school holidays

VARENGEVILLE-SUR-MER
On D75, 8 km west of Dieppe and 190 km from Calais

The exact location of Varengeville is vague, hard to pinpoint. In extremely pretty wooded country cut with deep little valleys, its houses and lanes are scattered among the verdure as if unconnected with one another. Indeed, it's not so much a village as an area of attractive houses and gardens, with many prosperous country homes glimpsed behind trees and hedges.

On the approach to the village (when coming from Calais), a sign points down a narrow lane to the Manoir d'Ango, a handsome sixteenth-century Renaissance mansion in black and white stone, unusual for its Italianate style, in the midst of restful countryside. The house is arranged around an impressive courtyard, and has a huge dovecote. It was the home of shipbuilder Jehan Ango who had his own fleet of corsairs – pirates – who gave some of their booty to the Crown. Ango became so wealthy in due course that not only did he build this fine château, but was in a position to lend money to the king, François I, who visited him here.

Then another sign shows the way down a lane to Parc des Moustiers. This cleverly laid-out botanic park covers 9 hectares, with rare trees, flowering bushes and sea views. It was mostly the work of the English landscape gardener Gertrude Jekyll. At its centre stands the unusual country house built by the great English imperial architect Sir Edwin Lutyens in 1898. It's fair, then, that the garden is described as an 'English-style park', though in fact quite formal by English standards. Paths lead among the bloom

and blossom, where glorious rhododendrons reach over
6 metres in height; and the arrowed walk changes according
to what is in flower (there's always something, from March
to November).

Beyond the Parc, the lane continues to a lonely parish
church, among lush greenery on the edge of a high cliff. Far
below it, waves roll on to a wide shore. Curving away into
the distance great white cliffs of Upper Normandy face the
sea. From this vantage point, Varengeville is not so much
sur mer as flying far above the sea and gazing down on it. A
graveyard surrounds the church, and some tombs seem on
the brink of crashing down into the water.

There are many interesting gravestones, among them
stones erected for men lost at sea. At one far corner of the
graveyard, in the most open and exposed position of all,
with a fantastic vista out to sea, a tall, striking, slender
monument in pink granite has only these words inscribed in
a naive, handwritten style (without capitals): 'marthe yard
1885–1968, reine yard 1914–1974, madeleine abeles, née
yard 1910–1936.'

*Varengeville:
The lonely parish
church overlooking
the sea*

But there are greater surprises. The eminent Cubist painter Georges Braque is buried here, together with his wife Marcelle, under a plain, pale slab. Some of his students made the blue and white mosaic headstone of a dove. Another grave, a huge, sculpted bronze box on a stone, is that of the distinguished composer Albert Roussel. On the stone, the epitaph he requested: 'It's facing the sea that we shall finish our existences and sleep to hear again from afar its eternal murmur.' A flat piece of grey stone teetering by the perimeter fence is the grave of mathematician Raphael Salem and his wife Adriana, with the beautiful epitaph, Montaigne's 'If I had to live again, I would live again as I have lived'. And on the other side of the church, the dramatist and poet Georges de Porto-Riche is buried.

The church dates from different periods, as can be seen instantly on stepping inside: two naves and two choirs have been welded together, one Romanesque with a barrel-vaulted roof and the other Gothic with a plain, wooden ridge. Round arches supported by strangely carved columns, one a spiral, one a hexagon, with odd figures in stone, separate the two. The older section is eleventh century, in pale, almost white stone; the later part, thirteenth and fifteenth century, partly brick, painted white. Beyond is a small, newer section, in brick. Three curiously primitive plaques on the wall date from the seventeenth century. Together with some older windows, there is superb modern stained glass. Especially notable is a Tree of Jesse in rich blues, the work of Georges Braque.

Manoir d'Ango grounds only open daily March–Nov.; rest of year, weekends and fêtes. Parc des Moustiers open March–Nov., a.m. and p.m., excluding Sun. a.m. House open for guided tours July–Aug.

CHAMPAGNE, ARDENNES, LORRAINE

Champagne, the former county which lies east of Paris and Picardy, is so varied in appearance and atmosphere that it seems reasonable to join it with other regions which provide further sharp contrasts. Predominantly flat or gently rolling, Champagne has a forested upland at its heart. Around the edges, it again becomes hillier and wilder, these hills at last climbing into the steeper, green slopes of Lorraine and the Ardennes. Yet the French Ardennes should not be likened to the Ardennes across the Belgian frontier. In France, the Ardennes are mere foothills, as the wooded slopes and plateaux of Lorraine, too, are foothills of the Vosges.

The whole region combines the twin blights of industry and war with attractive farm country and great expanses of wilderness contained within Regional Nature Parks. Northern Lorraine, in particular, is profoundly industrial, with mining, metalworks and chemical industries. Yet southern Lorraine enjoys pleasant spa resorts – Bains-les-Bains, Luxeuil-les-Bains, Plombières-les-Bains, Bourbonne-les-Bains – and natural springs whose waters are well known, such as Contrexeville and Vittel.

Few places, though, could be more appropriate for a celebration break than the quietly pretty Champagne country. As well as producing millions of bottles of the world's original 'bubbly' each year, the region has long been known for good living and fine cuisine. It's an excellent area for gentle touring and leisurely sightseeing.

Perhaps the biggest puzzle on reaching Champagne is the complete absence of vineyards. Where does the famous wine come from? Most of the vines are confined to the upland of the Montagne de Reims, and the Marne valley which flows along its southern edge. The rest of Champagne is soft, undulating, narrow fields of cereals and vegetables laid out like a modern painting on the pale, chalky soil. That, too, is very pleasing to the eye. The western edges of Champagne are green with little pastures in which contented cows stand and meditate. Their milk makes excellent cheeses, notably farm-fresh Brie.

The counts of Champagne, though independent, were always closely related to the crown of France. Their capital Reims, starting with Louis I in the year 816, was where all the kings of France were crowned. In 1284, the only child of Count Henri III, his daughter Jeanne, married Philippe le Bel, king of France. Champagne became officially united to France in 1361.

By contrast, Lorraine had a much more ambiguous relationship with France. In ancient times, after the division of Charlemagne's empire, it was a kingdom in its own right, with territories extending from the North Sea to Italy. This vast domain collapsed into two powerful duchies, one of which, Upper Lorraine, became the Lorraine of today. From 1048 right up to 1736 it was a duchy which

The Villages of Northern France

guarded a staunch independence from France, though towards the end of that period it was several times conquered and occupied by French forces. Its last duke was, curiously, Stanislas Leczinski, king of Poland. He was granted the Duchy of Lorraine only for his lifetime. When he died in 1766, Lorraine offically passed to the king of France. In 1871, as a result of the Franco-Prussian War, much of the duchy was seized by the Germans, who kept it until their defeat in 1918. It then became fully part of France.

The most important city in this part of northern France is Reims, directly accessible on the A26 from the Channel Tunnel, and still with a lot to recommend it. Reims Cathedral is a glorious Gothic masterpiece, replete with a sense of French history and nationhood. (Surprisingly, there's plenty of parking in the cobbled street and esplanade all around.) The outside has been badly damaged in parts, including the deep, elaborately carved main entrance, by bombs falling during both world wars. Yet if anything this seems to enhance the impression of something strong and beautiful which has stood up to the ravages of time.

Though outwardly a marvel of rich design, the cathedral is strangely bare inside. Treasures which were once displayed here, including gorgeous medieval tapestries, can be found next door in the Musée de Tau. Within a short stroll there's much more to see – historic buildings, bustling shopping

Looking across a sea of vineyards

streets, museums – while a drive to the suburbs brings you to some famous Champagne houses, such as Veuve Clicquot and Heidsieck.

If Reims is the capital of the Champagne region, the bustling town of Epernay is the capital of Champagne's wine. Most of the great Champagne makers – the *grandes marques* – are here. Their cellars extend along 200 kilometres of underground passages which thread the very ground on which Epernay stands. Many can be visited. Champagne Mercier, at 75 Avenue de Champagne, puts on a particularly interesting and entertaining free tour. In the far south of Champagne, Troyes is a large town with a delightfully picturesque old quarter of pedestrianized cobbled streets lined with timbered houses and mansions.

Nancy, the capital of Lorraine, though large and industrial, at its centre is one of the loveliest of towns. Cultured, civilized and with a city centre largely planned and built in the eighteenth century, it invites leisurely appreciation. The highlight is Place Stanislas, the ornately elegant main square enclosed by fine civic palaces of uniform design. It takes its name from Stanislas Leczinski, the Polish king who became the last duke of Lorraine. During his tenure, Nancy was grandly reconstructed. Elaborate, gilded wrought-iron gateways protect the entrances to the square, and similar ironwork can be seen in balcony railings on the grand buildings. The finest of these is the *hôtel de ville* whose sumptuous interiors

can be visited. From its first floor (up a superb staircase) you can enjoy the best view of the whole square. The adjacent Place de la Carrière also makes a grandiose set piece of eighteenth-century architecture. The town has some excellent art museums.

Metz, in northern Lorraine, has been an important fortified city and major river port on the confluence of the Seille and Moselle since the sixth century. Its defenses were legendary, a double ring of forts keeping a watchful guard around the city. In this century, it has become a focus of industry and commerce. At its centre, though, a good deal survives from the past, including a large number of fine churches and a majestic, late Gothic cathedral. The two rivers, with their islands, flanking the heart of the city give it a certain charm. There are several interesting museums.

In all the main cities of Champagne and Lorraine, outstanding restaurants can be found. Champagne, thanks to the influence of its sparkling wine, has drawn in chefs and specialities from all the surrounding provinces. Lorraine has a distinctive cuisine of its own, hearty, rich and meaty, with a preponderance of ham and pork, eggs, butter and cream. *Quiche Lorraine* is its great speciality, but the local version should not be likened to those poor imitations widely served elsewhere. *Potée* is a popular stew of pork meats and vegetables. *Charcuterie* and sausages are another local favourite. While better known for high-quality beers, Lorraine also produces its *vin gris*, a wine more pink than grey.

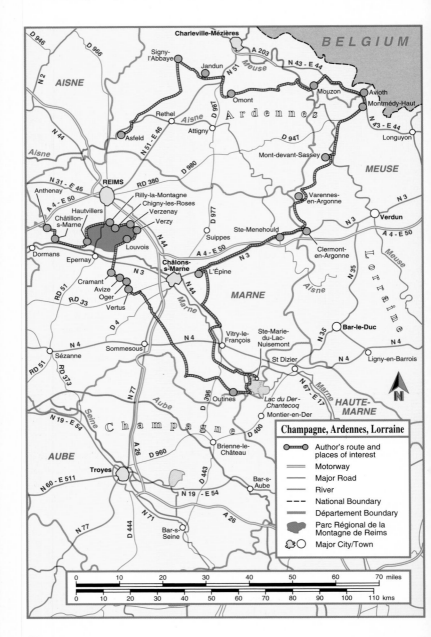

Champagne, Ardennes, Lorraine

- Author's route and places of interest
- Motorway
- Major Road
- River
- National Boundary
- Département Boundary
- Parc Régional de la Montagne de Reims
- Major City/Town

ANTHENAY
On D23 (off D380) 28 km southwest of Reims and 300 km from Calais

The village of Anthenay rises on a steep slope among high, open country with a wide view of large, rolling fields patched with sunlight and the shadow of clouds drifting overhead. In such a typical Champagne landscape there is not a vine to be seen, for most of the province consists of this spacious, gently undulating, arable farmland. Although so well known for its celebration wine, most of Champagne looks like this.

Anthenay is an attractive, rustic hamlet of stone cottages and farmhouses. On the lower side, fresh spring water pours from a pipe into a line of cattle troughs. A *lavoir* has been modernized and is still in use. Half way up the hill, a handsome little church with square stone belfry, stands within a walled churchyard. It dates from the twelfth century (with later work up to the sixteenth). Inside, with bare, pale stone, the church feels tiny and intimate.

At the top of the village, imposing walls enclose large grounds, suggesting a château. Look through the arched gateway, though, and discover only a simple farmyard. This is a good example of a fortified farmhouse, a *château-ferme*, a feature of Champagne's western borders.

CHÂTILLON-SUR-MARNE
Beside D1, 31 km southwest of Reims and 305 km from Calais

At last vineyards come within view, as the road reaches the valley of the Marne. On the slopes which rise from the river banks, the precious vines are arranged in neat, well-tended rows. An old fortified village poised on a ridge above the Marne, Châtillon gazes down on to Champagne vines on every side.

The village is most proud, though, of its gigantic statue of Pope Urban II, the man who created the concept of the Crusades and launched the First Crusade in 1096. It led to several more of these expeditions to the Holy Land, and to years of savagery and slaughter. Fighting under the flag of the Cross, the bloodthirsty adventurers – usually given a

The Villages of Northern France

Above:
*Stone cottages
climb to Anthenay's
twelfth-century
church*

Right:
*The immense
statue of
Pope Urban II
at Châtillon-sur-
Marne*

dispensation of forgiveness in advance for all sins committed – by the end had killed millions of people across Europe and the Middle East. The objective, successfully achieved, was to place Jerusalem under Christian rule and save it from Islam, which threatened to overtake and destroy the city's holy sites.

From the tiny triangular main 'square', Place Urbain II (where the bar, too, is named after the pious pope), take Rue de l'Église, a winding lane which passes the old church (notice the two bellringers' ropes hanging down inside the church), and a sign points the way to the statue. Of astonishing proportions, the granite figure, erected in 1887, stands in the middle of a little circular park at the summit of the hill, former site of a feudal castle. In season you can actually go inside the statue. Oddly enough, Urban II had no connections with Châtillon, having been born at Lagery, some 12 kilometres to the north.

Urban is shown bearded and crowned, draped in robes, and holding a cross up towards the surrounding countryside. He points to heaven with one finger. From here, Urban enjoys a panoramic view along the Marne and across the hills and flat fields of western Champagne.

HAUTVILLERS
On D386 (off N51) 25 km south of Reims and 300 km from Calais

Take the quieter north bank of the Marne, with vines on both sides of the road. Below, the river can be glimpsed, and on the far side, more vines. The scene in autumn is especially spectacular, either before the harvest when the champagne grapes hang waiting to be gathered, or after, when vine leaves take on every colour of the rainbow, red, yellow, purple, green, even hints of blue. On the approach to Epernay, the 'river' vineyards give way to the more distinguished 'mountain' vineyards which skirt the slopes of the Montagne de Reims.

The village looking over its vines
Poised on the southern slopes of the Montagne de Reims, looking across a glorious vista of vineyards into the

valley of the Marne and to the rooftops of Epernay, Hautvillers ranks as one of the most appealing villages in Champagne. Most of the vineyards surrounding it belong to Moët et Chandon.

It was here in Hautvillers that Dom Pérignon first created the much-imitated wine known everywhere in the world as champagne. For that reason, no doubt, there seems almost a touch of self-consciousness about Hautvillers, a degree of pride, that certainly is not undeserved. Quite apart from that important accident of history which occured here, the steep, angled lanes and streets of the little town are a delight, with flower boxes and dozens of exquisitely pretty corners. One striking feature is the large number of extraordinarily elaborate and interesting wrought-iron signs, mostly hanging over the premises of local champagne producers and merchants. Each one deserves inspection! Some of the most curious can be seen along Rue H. Martin, the village's main through-road, named for a Resistance member who died in German captivity.

Below and opposite: Wine makers' and merchants' elaborate wrought-iron signs

In the first years of the seventeenth century, Dom Pérignon was a blind cellarmaster at Hautvillers' Benedictine abbey. Clever with wine and vinification, he had often pondered whether more could be made of Champagne's local white wine which was naturally slightly petillant. During some experimentation he chanced upon the idea of a double fermentation in the bottle. On taking a first sip of the results he is said to have cried out: 'Come quickly – I'm drinking the stars!'

Now it's stars who drink Dom Pérignon. His old abbey church, Église St Sindulphe, has become the parish church of the village. Beside it, through huge, wooden gates, is the existing abbey. The entrance is in Square Beaulieu (named for the English village with which Hautvillers is twinned).

To make a tour of the Montagne de Reims, leave the village on D386, the Fismes road. Straight away the views

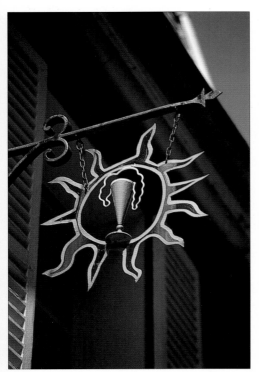

open up still more, with wonderful vistas across the vines and the Marne valley. The road follows the edge of the Montagne which has grapevines on its lower slopes and dense forest above. The whole of the Montagne de Reims is a protected Parc Régional, with paths and tracks cutting through the woodland. The road abandons the vines altogether for a while in the area of Nanteuil, after which take D22 to continue around the upland and rediscover the vineyard country, this time with views down towards the city of Reims.

RILLY-LA-MONTAGNE
On D26, 13 km south of Reims and 295 km from Calais

Most of the vineyard villages of the Montagne de Reims are remarkable only for their superb views and their wine. Apart from that they are workaday little places with plain and simple houses only adorned with a splash of colour from flowers at the windows. Often there may be an interesting church with a distinctive, ornate, black pointed spire, a feature of the area.

Between the villages, plaques at the corners of vine fields show which champagne *marque* – or name – they make. Many are famous, but there are plenty of unknown local names, too. Whatever their status, the vineyards are cared for attentively, and look immaculate. Occasionally, fields of other crops intervene as well. The wine road (D26) sometimes quits the vines altogether, briefly, to pass through the forest, another great resource both for villagers and visitors. The lovely woodlands make a striking contrast of scene and mood, and invite leisurely walks and drives.

On the edge of Rilly-la-Montagne, some charming, tiny vineyards grow on strange, steep hillocks. In the village centre, half-barrels planted with flowers have been placed prettily around the streets. Inside the village church, fine sixteenth-century sculpted choir stalls depict the vines and vine workers so important even then. Some attractive mansions can be seen here, several belonging to Rilly's many small champagne makers whose names for the most part are not familiar: signs proclaim champagne by Paques, Chauvet, Germain, Binet and many more. It's well worth buying. Unless you are a connoisseur, a bottle of champagne from a small producer tastes and feels as celebratory as one of the big names, yet costs just half the price.

Above the village, the slopes of Mont Joli offer some of the most enjoyable, easy walks among the woods of the Forêt de la Montagne.

CHIGNY-LES-ROSES
On D26, 14 km south of Reims and 296 km from Calais

A straightforward, hard-working wine village, Chigny lies within a veritable ocean of vines. In summer a mass of tender greenery, in autumn the leaves become spectacular with colour. A restored old wine press stands outside the premises of one of the champagne producers. Many of the houses, as if to live up to the charming name of the village, do indeed have roses clinging to them.

VERZENAY
On D26, 17 km south of Reims and 299 km from Calais

'Vineyards seem to pour down on to the houses'

Following D26 through the vines along the north slope of the Montagne de Reims, good views can be seen one after another. However, the approach to Verzenay gives grander vistas than most. Beside the road just before entering the

village, a windmill (property of Champagne Mumm, one of the great names) stands on a ridge surrounded by vines looking down towards Reims.

From this position, beside the mill, Verzenay itself looks striking. The village lies in a deep bowl of land lined with vineyards that seem to pour down on to the houses and streets. Yet this simple working village would be ordinary enough but for the view and the vines. A couple of Verzenay's champagne makers, Michel Arnould and Christian Busin, have *caves* (cellars) that can be visited.

VERZY
On D26, 19 km southeast of Reims and 301 km from Calais

A working village among the vines

For over one thousand years, from the seventh century to the eighteenth, the ancient vineyards of Verzy prospered under the care of a Benedictine abbey. The Revolution destroyed the abbey but the vines live on. Most of the fields all around the village now belong to Champagne Pommery,

one of the most prestigious names. Verzy is another busy, working village, attractively laid out with its triangular *place* in front of the *hôtel de ville*.

Take the Louvois road, D34, to reach the Faux de Verzy. Part of the forest which crowns the hillside above the village, the Faux is an area of weirdly misshapen, low beech trees (*faux*, in French meaning 'false', also means 'beech' in an old local patois, from the Latin for beech-woods, *fagus*). Paths for walkers and cyclists run through the Faux. Opposite the access road to the Faux, a footpath

leads 200 metres up the slopes of Mont Sinai to its summit (283 metres). This high point rises over the forest, the village and the vines, giving broad views over the Montagne and towards Reims. D34 continues downhill through woods and heath.

Twisted trees of the Faux de Verzy

LOUVOIS
On D9, 20 km south of Reims and 305 km from Calais

A stream, flowing in a deep channel, runs around and through quiet Louvois, on the southern edge of the Forêt de la Montagne de Reims. At the village centre, a thirteenth-century church has been attractively restored and stands, in a green churchyard with cropped trees, within an old walled enclosure.

At Louvois, the daughters of Louis XV had a 'holiday home' in the form of a splendid château originally built by Mansart for Louis XIV. Although much of the château was destroyed in the early nineteenth century, what remained has been handsomely restored. This grand residence in pale

Louvois: the elegant château

stone, still privately owned, stands on what is now the main road to Reims. Although the château cannot be visited, it makes an imposing sight, standing in its wooded park, even if you only pause to admire it through the ornate black gateway.

D9 heads towards the River Marne and busy champagne capital Epernay, on the way passing the village of Avenay-Val-d'Or, with its flamboyant church. If you want to by-pass Epernay, at Mareuil-sur-Aÿ – which despite the name is on the bank of the Marne – D9 crosses the river and runs across flat country directly towards the next champagne vineyard area, the Montagne d'Epernay.

CRAMANT
On D10, 20 km south of Reims and 305 km from Calais

The Montagne d'Epernay, like the Montagne de Reims, combines green forest on the higher ground and golden vineyards lower down. Along its eastern edge projects a long, high ridge of white chalk planted with white Chardonnay grapes. That's why this escarpment is called the Côte Blanche, or Côte des Blancs. Its grapes are

Cramant: champagne is its life and soul

destined for the finest champagnes and those called Blanc des Blancs, and its wine villages are small, prosperous, often picturesque, and give good views across the vines, the plain, the valley and the upland beyond.

Cramant, in an especially attractive position, has just the right conditions of soil, humidity and sunlight to specialize in a Chardonnay variety which has won particular renown, Pinot Blanc Chardonnay. Vineyards drape the slopes above and descend right into the heart of the village. Most belong to Moët et Chandon. Yet despite its prestige, Cramant remains a simple, working, farming community of ordinary brick and stone houses. Wine making is its life and soul. At the entrance to the village, in a *place*, stands a restored old wine press. In the main square, Place Puisard, the post office and *mairie* are both adorned with carved stone plaques depicting grapes.

AVIZE
On D10, 22 km south of Reims and 307 km from Calais

Along this chalky ridge, the villages lie one beside the other, and it's only about 4 kilometres from Cramant to another distinguished neighbour. There are more superb views near Avize, especially from the hillside above. Vineyards come into the edges of this long, thin village noted for excellent grapes and champagne. Several small champagne houses can be found here, together with a champagne wine-making college.

The village appears deeply preoccupied with work, and has earned its prosperity. In the quiet main square, Place Léon Bourgeois, there's a fountain, some trees and several champagne makers. The unusual parish church has three gables on one side, two on the other. Though originally twelfth century, it has gargoyles projecting and other distinctive later Gothic features.

OGER
On D10, 24 km south of Reims and 309 km from Calais

Even less distance brings you to the next great wine village of the Côte Blanche, barely 2 kilometres away. Flowers growing everywhere make Oger charming. They burst out beside the streets and in tubs and in the main square. Here, too, are small champagne houses and an interesting old church, twelfth and thirteenth century, with a high, square tower.

Just two more kilometres takes the road to next-door Le Mesnil-sur-Oger. Though less attractive, the big round corner tower of Champagne Launois makes a striking entrance to this long and narrow wine-making village. There's an unusual church – spanning the centuries from Romanesque to Renaissance – and a pleasing main square.

*The vineyards
prepare for winter ...*

*... and flourish in
high summer*

The Villages of Northern France

VERTUS

On D9, 30 km south of Reims and 315 km from Calais

At the southern end of the Côte des Blancs, Vertus is an agreeable small town. On first sight, especially from the passing main road, there seems little to stop for. Stroll in the old centre, though, and its unpretentious charm, its pleasant little squares and old curiosities will soon be revealed.

The town's long history has been dominated by the vine. Today, the *commune* possesses 450 hectares of champagne vineyards, and several champagne makers can be found among its winding streets. Yet this is not a prime site for high-quality vines, and Vertus does not have the air of comfortable prosperity possessed by other villages higher on the Côte des Blancs.

A broad avenue, almost without traffic, encircles the old centre: it runs along former defenses that lay just outside the town walls, for Vertus was once fortified. It even had a château, belonging to the Counts of Champagne. But of the fortifications nothing remains, and of the château, only a single gateway called Porte Baudet.

Start at the main square, Place Léon Bourgeois. In the *place* an ornate fountain stands in front of an enticing *pension-bar-restaurant* (called Café des Arts) in an old house fortified with a corner turret. Streets and lanes leading off are lined with houses and cottages almost all of which have concealed their age behind modern façades. Uncovered (as just a few are), the houses are of fine, pale stone, and the cottages of picturesque wattle and daub.

Rue Général Koenig leads to the surviving gateway, and from there Rue de l'Église brings you to no ordinary village church. The Église de St Martin de Vertus makes a striking impression for four reasons: its age, its size, its beauty, and the great neglect from which it suffers. Originally dating back perhaps some 1,200 years into the the Merovingian (pre-Romanesque) period, the church was rebuilt sometime between 1000 and 1100 by a community of canons. Damaged by fire in 1167, it was repaired and became simply the parish church of Vertus. Although altered and repaired over the centuries, the impression given remains predominantly that of the stately and dignified

Romanesque, with rounded arches rising up a sturdy square tower.

Inside, later periods are more in evidence. A sense of space and light is created by the wide central nave and some beautiful stained glass. There is early Gothic vaulting, and four Gothic arches pierce what is almost a wall separating the aisles. There's some good sixteenth-century statuary, and in the dark, narrow transept, some modern glasswork. Steps lead down to four ancient crypts. Unfortunately, the church is terribly damp and would also benefit from a thorough cleaning.

The damp could be due to the underground river which bursts out at several places in Vertus. Steps lead down beside the church to a large pool of it behind the building. Known as the Puits St Martin, enclosed within fine stonework, the water is perfectly clear and clean. Ducks and swans swim about, while to one side stands the open-sided structure which once housed a *lavoir*. Handsome stone houses, set back, form a square around the pool.

Interesting little squares, one joining another, are a feature of the town. Walk downhill from the church to Place de la Fontaine. The *fontaine* is a small pool of fast flowing water enclosed by stone walls, with steps down at each corner. Wrought ironwork, decorated with flowers, encloses the fountain, which in the past was considered to have medicinal, perhaps even magical, qualities.

That square gives way to another, called simply Rue de l'Hôtel-Dieu. On the near corner stands a timbered house, while in the far corner the town's *mairie* occupies the old *hôtel-Dieu*, with a courtyard enclosed by ornate railings bearing an odd crest: a heart shot through with an arrow.

Vertus lies at the limits of northern Champagne and the picturesque wine country. Beyond to the south, the landscape changes to become extraordinarily featureless, the flatness revealing nothing but immense fields without hedges, only occasionally relieved by a copse of trees.

OUTINES

On D55, 111 km southeast of Reims and 386 km from Calais

Beyond the flat lands of southern Champagne, in the south-eastern corner of the old duchy, attractive areas reappear with gentle hills, woods and lakes. The shores of the huge artificial Lac du Der-Chantecoq, created in 1974 to regulate the flow of the capricious River Marne, has become a popular place for outdoor activities and short breaks. The region around the lake has preserved much of its traditional character. Some of the villages are delightful with their old wood-framed houses. On the northern shore, Ste-Marie-du-Lac-Nuisement, which barely escaped submersion within the new lake, has become a museum of the former life of the district. On the other side of the water, Châtillon-sur-Broué and, especially, Outines are two small neighbours, living villages which retain an ensemble of timbered dwellings, greenery and flowers, and a church with a black stiletto spire of wooden tiles.

Timberwork detail at Outines

Museum-village, Ste-Marie-du-Lac-Nuisement open April–June; Sept. weekends and fêtes p.m. only; July–Aug. p.m. daily

The half-timbered church at neighbouring Châtillon-sur-Broué

L'ÉPINE
On N3, 55 km southeast of Reims and 320 km from Calais

Here in the eastern part of the region, on the border of Lorraine, the Champagne countryside becomes mild, gently undulating, laid out in strips of neat farmland where grain and vegetables grow. Once more, grapes have disappeared from the scene.

Few villages better convey the sense of the area's quiet prosperity and civilization than flowery little L'Épine. At its heart is a broad, open *place*, triangular, enclosed by simple, well-kept houses. But this tranquil spot has made its mark on the world. Above all, the village is dominated by two shrines. One, the glorious Basilica of Notre Dame, soars grandly from one end of the *place*. This vast cathedral in pale stone is the perfect example of rich Gothic ornamentation; it is similar to the cathedral in Reims, though with the addition of attractive galleried towers. Note, too, the intriguing gargoyles. The interior is lofty and inspiring, especially if you happen to arrive when the organist is practising and the air resounding with music.

For centuries, pilgrims – including kings – streamed here, for the basilica marks the spot where some shepherds supposedly came across a statue of the Virgin in a burning bush.

L'Épine's other shrine is to gastronomy. In the *place*, on a corner, stands the hotel-restaurant Aux Armes de Champagne. Its restaurant, in several rooms, has an air of enjoyment and opulence, precision and perfectionism, Here latter-day pilgrims come to pay homage to fine cooking and great wines. The *patron*, Monsieur Perardel, runs a good wine shop in atmospheric *caves* where all the *grandes marques* of Champagne can be bought at good prices. It seems fitting enough that Monsieur Perardel is also L'Épine's long-standing mayor.

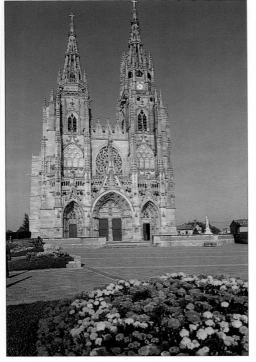

The village is remarkably easy to get to, thanks to the uncrowded A26 *autoroute* which runs direct from Calais to Châlons, leaving just a pleasant, short drive towards the basilica rising from the surrounding countryside.

The Basilica of Notre Dame, L'Épine

STE-MENEHOULD

On N3, 73 km east of Reims and 350 km from Calais

This busy little town (its name is pronounced Sant Menould) marks the beginning of Lorraine. Beyond it lie the forests of Argonne. In one way, though, it has a vital Champagne connection: here in 1638 Dom Pérignon was born, destined to invent the *méthode champenoise* which would make Champagne synonymous with celebration. The upper town stands atop a steep ridge, and is known as Le Château. It has a villagey appeal, with its old, timbered houses decorated with flowers. There's a good view across the lower town and the Aisne valley. The handsome village church, of the thirteenth and fifteenth centuries, is made of striped brick and stone.

The same idea is repeated on a grander scale in the lower town, the highlight of which – though cut through by the *route nationale* – is its central square, Place Général Leclerc. The *place* is dominated by the stately *hôtel de ville* constructed

Ste-Menehould's church

The stately main square in Ste-Menehould's lower town

in 1730 in alternating stripes of brick and stone. Here on 21 June 1791, as they attempted to flee France, Louis XVI and Marie-Antoinette were recognized by J. B. Drouet, the son of the postmaster of nearby Varennes, who had only ever seen the king's likeness before on the head of a six-livre coin. He rushed ahead to Varennes (see below), where he raised the alarm and preparations were made to arrest the royal couple.

CLERMONT-EN-ARGONNE
On N3, 88 km east of Reims and 365 km from Calais

The gently undulating Argonne, western border of Lorraine, is a varied patchwork of grain and vegetables, pasture and a considerable area of forest. Its unfortunate destiny has been as the battlefront in several conflicts, most notably during the Great War when a bloodily contested stretch of front line ran across the region. From nearly flat countryside rises a strangely steep, little hill: on and below it lies the village of Clermont.

Its humble central square, Place de la République, is dominated by memories of war. A single large wall has been dedicated as a war memorial, while another unusual plaque is dedicated to the Deported Martyrs. These were the 100 local men who, on 30 July 1944, were transported to the Nazis' extermination camps. Twenty-seven escaped death but seventy-three died, innocent victims, as the plaque states, of German 'barbarians'.

From the *place*, a lane mounts steeply to a delightful sixteenth-century church in golden stone, with a tower fortification topped by an elaborate black belfry. Double Renaissance doorways almost give it the appearance of a grand house rather than a church. Inside, the choir and transept are in flamboyant Gothic style, while the stained glass includes good modern work. From beside the building there is a wide view across woods and fields rippling away into the distance. Continue down the lane which climbs the hill to arrive at a little chapel, Ste Anne, standing on the site of a former château. It contains a fine sixteenth-century Holy Sepulchre with six statues.

VARENNES-EN-ARGONNE
On D38, 88 km east of Reims and 365 km from Calais

Either travel directly north from Clermont to Varennes on the straight road through flat country, or retrace your steps to one of the forest roads. In the woods, remnants of the First World War – trenches and other earthworks – can still be seen. West of Varennes, the Abris de Kronprinz is a German bunker used by the Crown Prince of Germany during the battles. Almost opposite, D38c leads through the trees to a monument to the dead of Argonne, and a military cemetery.

Arriving at the edge of Varennes, D38 passes a museum in an ugly, single-storey, modern building; displays inside cover the three principal strands in the story of the village: the arrest of Louis XVI, the Great War, and the production of high-quality porcelain.

Beside the museum rises the imposing memorial, a huge, white monument with high columns, erected in 1927 to honour the troops of the State of Pennsylvania who liberated this area. The memorial opens to an immense vista, looking across the River Aire to a quiet, rustic landscape of woods, fields and pasture.

Descend a few paces from the American memorial to reach

The River Aire at Varennes

the little Place de l'Hôtel de Ville, where a fountain full of flowers stands on one side of the road and the Tour Louis XVI on the other. This simple, stone tower replaces the original belfry, burned down by the Germans, which marked the spot where on 21 June 1791, sometime between 11 p.m. and midnight, Louis XVI and the royal family were arrested by J. B. Drouet and taken under guard to the fortress of Montmédy (see below). Having spotted the king at Ste-Menehould, Drouet had ridden ahead of the royal carriage to organize assistance for his capture.

The tower looks down upon the Aire as it pours through the simple village centre.

Museum open April–June, and Oct. weekdays p.m., weekends a.m. and p.m.; July–Sept. a.m. and p.m. daily

MONT-DEVANT-SASSEY
Off D964, 100 km east of Reims and 375 km from Calais

Rising and falling to meet little rivers, winding between and through areas of woodland, D998 makes its way across Lorraine countryside to the Meuse valley. On the lower

slope of a hill rising from the river, little Mont-devant-Sassey enjoys a tranquil, pastoral setting. It is noted especially for a majestic fortified church. The great grey building among the trees, looking down on to the red-roofed village, stands on a beautiful eleventh-century crypt. The rest of the church underwent numerous additions and alterations, especially in the Gothic thirteenth century.

The fortified church and the village

MONTMÉDY-HAUT
Off N43, 61 km from Charleville-Mezières and 300 km from Calais

Travel north through Lorraine's Ardennes foothills towards the Belgian border. From the modern, main-road village of Montmédy, a steep narrow lane winds upward to its lonely, historic neighbour Montmédy-Haut. Enclosed within the high walls of a mighty hilltop citadel, the older village makes an impressive sight from below.

To enter the ancient fortress you must cross two moats via narrow drawbridges, and pass through a narrow, curved tunnel within the huge ramparts. The drawbridges are still workable, and wooden gates still hang on the gateways.

Though outwardly so imposing, within the walls the village feels small, remote, quiet. There is so little traffic that birds can be heard singing. A fine church and a few houses of crumbling, golden sandstone stand around the sides of a deserted central square. A few lanes lead away from the square to peaceful rows of houses beside well-tended gardens. The surrounding ramparts are the dominating presence, so high that they cut off any sense of what lies beyond them.

Today, beside the main gateway, a tourist office provides information about this old stronghold and its history: a medieval fortress, it suffered frequent attacks, sometimes rebuffing them, sometimes being taken captive. Becoming a border town of France, it was given (by Vauban, Louis XIV's innovative military engineer) the greater fortifications that survive now. Even in this century it has seen action – the very last shots of the Great War were fired from here.

Next to the tourist office, a doorway opens into an eerie corridor of stone descending beneath the walls. We followed it down, along stone tunnels and steps, to emerge on the other side of the inner rampart. The tourist office also gives access to a walkway on top of the ramparts. Walking around them gives a clear view of the power and complexity of Montmédy's double ring of defenses reinforced by six stout bastions. From this position the setting is striking: an immense vista of attractive, wooded hills, the French and Belgian Ardennes, spreads into the far distance.

Winter comes to the fortress village of Montmédy-Haut

AVIOTH
On D110, 62 km east of Charleville-Mézières and 288 km from Calais

The country lane wanders among a peaceful Ardennes landscape of high rolling farmland, copses, and fields enclosed by mature hedges.

Suddenly, two magnificent spires rise up from the pastures. They stand on the beautiful elaborate Gothic church of Avioth, an astonishing sight in so rustic a setting. This would be, in any case, a delightful farming village on a hilltop, its old stone houses and farmyards in terraces surrounded by their fields. From here, lovely views extend far into the farms and woods of these green, tranquil hills.

The church, at the centre of the little village, seems at first to be a marvellous eccentricity. A superb, skilful piece of Gothic architecture, it looks quite out of place. The main south portal is wonderfully carved, and contains a multitude of figures as well as sculpted draperies 'hanging' on either side of the entrance.

Avioth: a great, Gothic basilica in a simple farming village

In front stands a small, exquisite, hexagonal structure in flamboyant Gothic style. Open to the elements, uncared-for, this contains an ancient wooden carving of the Madonna

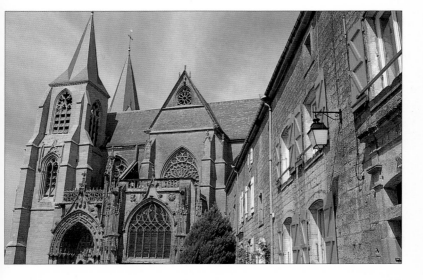

and Child. Known as La Recevresse, this tiny building is where pilgrims leave offerings on arriving at the church. For the church at Avioth is not a mere eccentricity, but holds another wooden carving of the Madonna and Child, revered as miraculous, the object of pilgrimage for centuries.

Twin narrow doorways enter the soaring golden nave. Yet the interior is much smaller than expected. The floor is of bare stone; the walls, though elaborately carved, are unadorned; the ceiling is rib-vaulted, especially beautiful above the choir with its seven Gothic arches, and good stained glass includes a fine rose window. In the choir, the painted carving of Notre Dame d'Avioth and Child is draped in white. She was found in the eleventh century and the present church was constructed for her 200 years later.

On the other side of the church square, the bar À la Recevresse provides tourist information as well as refreshments and an excellent view.

MOUZON
On D19 and D964, 43 km east of Charleville-Mezières and 277 km from Calais

Mouzon keeps its charm

Mouzon's *zone industrielle* is rather too apparent. Yet the place manages to keep its appeal. The attractive and interesting

thirteenth-century abbey church, with its two later spires, conserves the town's charm. The portal of the church, very richly carved, opens into an impressive, spacious interior with massive round pillars and high galleries. The finely carved wooden organ loft is from the eighteenth century.

All around the church are pleasing squares with fountains and old houses in pale stone. The setting, beside the River Meuse, is rustic. But the town has a long history of industry. Its main product, felt, is all explained in the Musée du Feutre, where ancient and modern felt work is on show, and there are hands-on displays allowing visitors a chance to try some felt making themselves. The museum is situated in what was once the abbey farm, but the abbey has gone, leaving this as a likeable town of both tractors and factory chimneys.

Museum of Felt open daily July–Aug. a.m. and p.m.; June, Sept. p.m. only; May, Oct. weekends p.m. only

OMONT
On D33, 27 km south of Charleville-Mezières and 240 km from Calais

High in the midst of woods, tiny Omont possesses little but its glorious views. From one side, a hill rises steeply, its trees pressing against the back walls of old village houses. On the other side, the slope falls away sharply into a valley, with a broad landscape of fields where sheep and cows meditate.

The hamlet has a mix of large old stone dwellings, some almost collapsing with age, and smaller new homes put up by people attracted to this magnificent setting. Mature orchards and patches of pasture on the village boundary are being saved from falling into abandonment by the newcomers.

Once, though it seems unimaginable, this was an important town, a fortified stronghold of the local nobility, and an ecclesiastical centre. A château stood on the summit of its hill. Held by the anti-Protestant Catholic League during the vicious Wars of Religion, it was beseiged and taken in 1591 by no less a general than Henri IV in person.

Of those days hardly even memories remain, except for one odd anomaly: Omont officially retains its archaic position as the district's capital town.

The Villages of Northern France

Between the valleys of the Meuse and the Aisne rises a last gentle range of Ardennes hills, gorgeously green and pastoral, known as Les Crêtes. It's a marvellous little corner of countryside perfect for easy, unhurried walks and drives. It's almost unknown to outsiders, and many of the villages are like gems undiscovered and unpolished. Jandun is one of them.

On the edge of the village, spacious well-made houses of fine honey-coloured stone are arranged haphazardly on either side of the through-road. Many are farmhouses with their enclosed yards. Alongside the roadway broad, grassy verges lie like a carpet beneath the shade of tall chestnut trees. All around spreads a quiet, satisfying landscape of rolling meadows and pasture.

A village of handsome stone houses

Turn away from the road to find the heart of the village. The same solid, handsome houses of pale stone, set behind a

wide verge of clipped grass, line a couple of streets. Beside most of them, large stacks of firewood await the end of summer. The Gothic church on its grassy hill stands at the top of the village. At the end of the main street, a useful signboard shows marked walks in Les Crêtes.

SIGNY L'ABBAYE
On D27 and D985, 54 km southwest of Charleville-Mézières and 221 km from Calais

The extensive Forêt de Signy covers the uplands of both sides of the little River Vaux with fine woodland of oak, beech and rowan. Lanes and paths make enjoyable tours among the trees. Modest curiosities and sights are signposted: an ancient tree, a deposit-encrusted fountain, a waterside château. Against the wooded hillsides of the Forêt nestle the black rooftops of Signy.

Once, Signy was a Cistercian monastery, founded by St Bernard of Cîteaux himself in 1134, but it was completely destroyed in the Revolution. The village which grew around it survives as an unassuming little country town, bustling and lively, of simple brick and stone houses. Through its centre flows the canalized River Vaux.

The main street, Place Aristide Briand, climbs the gentle slope from the river and the tall grey church, up to the fine *mairie*, standing on the arches of a small covered marketplace. On the corner opposite the *mairie*, the solid provincial Auberge de l'Abbaye offers good set menus and decent rooms.

The town's oddity is the Gibergeon at the corner of Rue de Thin and Rue de Rocroi. This crater-like hole in the ground, hidden among an untidy clump of trees, is a natural spring. It forms a strange circular pond (its area is about 10 square metres, and the depth is around 12 metres) from which water pours down through the town centre into the Vaux.

The Villages of Northern France

ASFELD
On D926, 26 km north of Reims and 275 km from Calais

The curious village church

Returning across the gently undulating fields of southern Ardennes and northern Champagne towards Reims, pause at this little town beside the River Aisne. It possesses a remarkable church, built in 1683. A strange, elaborate edifice, all of brick, it is a mass of weird cupolas and curves, pillars and porticos.

ALSACE

Love of tradition is the hallmark of Alsace. By good fortune, it happens to be a land whose traditions possess exceptional charm. Everything about the place is curiously distinctive – language, food and wine, feasts and festivals, the look of the houses. Through the centuries that Alsace has been batted from France to Germany, Germany to France, the people of Alsace have clung tenaciously to their own customs and culture.

The many German visitors imagine that they see a piece of Germany that has come adrift and been lost to France. They consider its ancient patois as a brand of German (it resembles Swiss German), and consider the Germanic style of cooking as the final proof of the true identity of the Alsatians. They could not be more wrong. Few other regions of France are as staunchly proud of their French nationality as Alsace.

Yet to reach it, you must first cross the Vosges mountains. In the past, the barrier they present helped to preserve the character of Alsace. The Vosges is a wild, forested landscape, yet one where – on the Lorraine side – industry and wartime damage have deprived most towns and villages of their appeal. Suddenly the road reaches the summits and the borders of Alsace, then descends through the hills to the vast valley plain. Through this flat land flows the Rhine and, parallel to the larger river, the River Ill which gives Alsace its name (called Ellsass by locals). All at once, the towns and villages are a delight, nearly every village a chocolate-box picture.

Most striking is the fairy-tale cottage architecture. The houses stand a solid timber frame on a base of large stones, the massive beams arranged in a distinctive pattern with main timbers going off at an angle. Between the beams, wattle and daub is caked on thickly and painted bright, pastel colours. They look like the work of bakers, not builders. Roofs are tall and steep, and many village houses have huge, gaping archways into ground-floor storage or work areas or cobbled courtyards. Lintels, corner timbers and doorposts are decorated and carved, sometimes with ancient designs and symbols, and window ledges brightly arrayed with an abundance of flowers.

Even new buildings have an eye to the traditional style, because the people of Alsace have such strong ideas as to how things should look and how things should be done, and they cling to these customs tenaciously. The result is almost a superfluity of delightful little towns and villages. Dozens of them that might be included on our itinerary had they been in any other region, have simply been left out. Here we have concentrated on the Wine Road, which follows the slope of the Rhine and Ill valley. Up in the Vosges peaks, many other gems can be discovered by those who wish to explore further. North of Strasbourg, as the hills reach up towards the German border, a dozen more exquisite villages reward a visit. It's not hard to find attractive villages anywhere in Alsace – though few have anything to be said about them except that they are astonishingly picturesque.

To either side of the *Route des Vins* (the Wine Road) perfectly maintained vines grow high on neat sticks and wires. So high are the plants that in places they tower over the road. Labourers, even tractors, can disappear without trace into the foliage. On the hillsides, the vineyards climb towards the forested summits, while on the valleyside they slope down gently to the broad, hazy plain. In the distance, the mass of the mountains often

A storks' nest on the point of a tower – storks are the ancient symbol of Alsace

appears blue. The vineyards themselves, a tender, pale green for much of the year, become a kaleidoscope of rainbow colours in the autumn just after the harvest.

Does Alsace belong in France or Germany? The disagreement goes back a long time. Gauls believed that the Rhine was their frontier, but the Teutons considered the summit of the Vosges to be the border. The Celts living between the Vosges and the Rhine endured constant harrassment by Teutonic raiders. The Romans, when they took over, agreed with the Gauls.

With the fall of Rome, Germanic tribes took turns to invade and devastate the land until Charlemagne set the border along the Rhine. When his empire was divided between his three sons, Alsace and Lorraine remained together. In the ninth century, Alsace came under German rule. It was to remain outside France for 800 years – but for most of that time was not part of Germany either. Instead, its ten largest towns were united in the Decapole, a self-governing confederation. The rural areas were in the hands of local lords. However, German influence on Alsace during this period gave the region its Germanic character.

The Thirty Years War (1618–1648) between Catholic and Protestant forces for control of central Europe left Germany and Alsace devastated. France, becoming the dominant power in Europe, took possession of Alsace. So it remained until, with the unification of Germany in 1870, the Prussians declared war on France. They marched into Alsace and Lorraine, clinging on to those territories until the end of the First World War.

The Alsatians greatly resented this German occupation and maintained a constant state of rebellion. One of the heroes of the time was Uncle Hansi (Jean-Jacques Waltz), painter and caricaturist, whose grotesque mockery of the Germans and glorification of all things French and Alsatian remain popular even today (he died as recently as in 1951). You'll often see prints of his drawings on postcards: notice the signature HANSI in one corner.

Eventually, in 1918, Alsace rejoined France. But in the Second World War, Germany again seized Alsace. The Nazi way of convincing the Alsatians to love their German heritage was a catalogue of repressive legislation. The use of Alsace dialect or French, or French names, was strictly forbidden. Thousands of Alsatians were sent to Le Struthof concentration camp in the Vosges for lack of German patriotism (10,000 died there), while the region's large Jewish population was efficiently rounded up for mass extermination. Not surprisingly, the people of Alsace rejoiced in 1945 when Germany was defeated and the region again became part of France. Alsatians also take delight that their cosmopolitan capital, Strasbourg, has become the seat of the Council of Europe and European Parliament, which to many of them symbolises the end of the German problem.

Strasbourg – since ancient time a meeting of highways, as the name implies – is a dynamic, thriving city, forward-looking yet preserving a great heritage. Two branches of Alsace's river, the Ill, entirely enclose the historic central district. Several other meandering canalized waterways give something of the same appeal to districts between the city centre and the Rhine, which skirts Strasbourg's eastern edge. To the west rises the blue horizon of the Vosges summits. On the western tip of the city's island centre, the former artisans' neighbourhood La Petite France conserves a charming tangle of lanes, old houses and covered bridges.

Focal point of the city is its superb cathedral and the ancient district around the building. Construction of the Cathédrale Notre Dame, on a site which had been regarded as sacred by Romans and by Celts before them, and upon which a church had been erected by Charlemagne, began in 1015 in pure Romanesque style. Yet by 1439, when the building was completed, the cathedral had become a masterpiece of pure Gothic architecture. A fantastic array of fine statuary and tracery adorns the façade and portal on the west side.

One of the doorways carries beautiful carvings of the Wise and Foolish Virgins. An elegant lofty spire of fine Gothic open-work, flanked by four turrets, soars high above the city.

Inside, exquisite stained glass enhances a vast nave of satisfying proportions. There's an eighteenth-century Silbermann organ, and a fascinating astronomical clock which springs into activity every day at noon. Stairs lead down to the eleventh-century crypt.

The Villages of Northern France

Between the cathedral and the riverside several imposing buildings can be seen, notably the huge, eighteenth-century Château des Rohan which houses three distinguished museums of fine arts, history, and ceramics. Strasbourg has many other first-class museums.

Colmar, a smaller city further south, preserves much warm Alsace atmosphere in its historic central quarter. Its streets and squares of typically ornate and elaborately timbered dwellings and civic buildings are a delight. It, too, has several good museums, especially the Musée d'Unterlinden in a former thirteenth-century convent. Many outstanding paintings can be seen, ranging from medieval religious works to such twentieth-century artists as Picasso and Braque.

The two cities lie at each end of our vineyard route. On the way, other country towns of Alsace deserve a pause. Sélestat, for example, keeps its medieval central district, and has an interesting museum (the Bibliothèque Humaniste) of books and manuscripts dating back to the seventh century. Heading into the Vosges uplands, Gérardmer (pronounced Gerarmé) is one of the most popular resort towns in Alsace. Although with some industry and almost entirely modern since being rebuilt after destruction by the Germans in the last war, it has a wonderful lakeside location and is ideally placed for walking or driving in the scenic hill country all around.

Despite a certain Germanic style, and German terminology which misleads visitors, the food of Alsace ranks among the best in France.

Michelin rosettes and Gault Millau toques have been liberally sprinkled over the whole region. Goose fat and pork fat feature strongly in the cooking, *charcuterie* and sausages reach the highest quality, and *pâtés*, too, are a strong point here. Chicken cooked in Alsace wine, with mushrooms and cream, is a delicate favourite of the region. The greatest Alsace speciality is sauerkraut, though known by its French name of *choucroute*, made with wine and served with sausage. River fish from the Vosges, particularly trout, appear on most menus. Try a wedge of strong, local Munster cheese. Puddings, too, make a good showing at the Alsace table. Rich fruit pies and tarts are especially popular. *Kougelhopf*, a proud Alsace tradition, is the distinctively shaped fruitcake that mixes cream, eggs and sugar into a yeasted dough with raisins and almonds. It can be lighter or heavier, more or less fruity, and appears at any and every opportunity. The name varies, sometimes becoming *kougelhof* or *koilopf*.

It's not unusual, though, for things Alsatian to be known by a variety of names and accents, because the Alsace patois has its own local variations. For example, the *winstubs* of Strasbourg become *wistubs* in Colmar. These convivial eating and drinking establishments invite you to abandon your privacy and reserve, and sit down at jolly shared tables to enjoy some good Alsatian home-cooking and a glass of local wine.

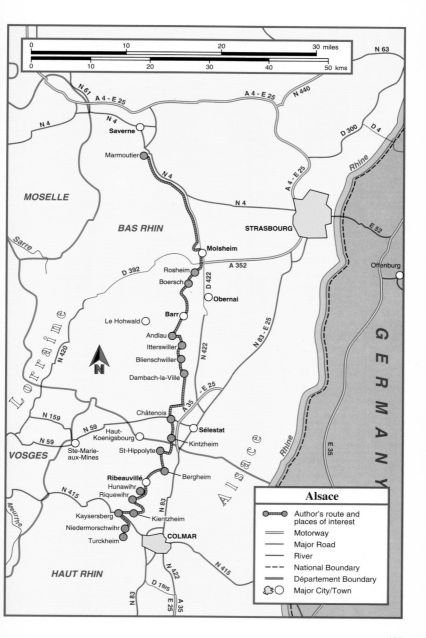

Alsace

	Author's route and places of interest
	Motorway
	Major Road
	River
	National Boundary
	Département Boundary
	Major City/Town

The Villages of Northern France

MARMOUTIER
Off N4, 38 km from Strasbourg and 583 km from Calais

Having crossed the Vosges mountains, *autoroute* A4 descends into the Alsace plain at Saverne. Take the Saverne exit and, by-passing the region's capital Strasbourg, travel southward into the picturesque rural heartland of Alsace. Marmoutier, a hard-working little town just beyond Saverne, cannot be counted among the jewels of the region, but it makes a worthwhile pause. Around its central square, Place Général de Gaulle, there are some fine old houses of timber and stone, an ornate old fountain, a hotel and restaurant.

It also has one of the most magnificent examples of Romanesque art in Alsace. Standing right across the end of the *place*, filling the width of the square, the monumental façade of Marmoutier's abbey church presents a thrilling spectacle. The stone itself, gorgeous yellow and red ochres cut into fine blocks, is especially striking. Three arches on round pillars pierce the façade and form the entrance to the vaulted porch where the theme of three arches is repeated. The imposing frontage is decorated in the Lombard style, that is to say, it is quite flat and ornamented only with mock carved pillars and a frieze of rounded arch motifs. It rises to three gables standing before three towers: one large square in the middle flanked by two lovely octagonal towers.

An abbey was founded here at the beginning of the seventh century by Leobard, a disciple of the Irish missionary Columban. It prospered and grew, erecting the present church in the twelfth century (the façade and towers date from around 1150). Inside, a more ancient crypt can be seen. However, much of the interior of the church was rebuilt in the sixteenth century. There's a Silbermann organ of 1710. The abbey itself was broken up at the Revolution.

The next pause on the journey south will be at another Romanesque masterpiece. Press on through attractive country along N4, perhaps stopping after 5 kilometres at the village of Romanswiller, just off the highway, to see the Jewish cemetery in which graves date from the fifteenth century. After Wasselone, leave the busy *route nationale* and take D422, towards Molsheim and the wine country.

ROSHEIM

On D35, 30 km from Strasbourg and 614 km from Calais

D422 first reaches the town of Molsheim, with its charming old fortified centre rising from the River Bruche, and continues southward, passing some industry. Leave the road by turning right on to D35 which reaches Rosheim after just 5 kilometres.

A wide main street runs from one end to the other of this small town, passing through fortified gateways at either end and, in the middle, running beneath a long dwelling which spans the road. In all, three gates of the once staunchly defended town have survived: Lion, Basse and École. Along the broad high street, both within and without the gateways, a number of picturesque old houses can be seen. Among them are some of the most ancient in Alsace, including the Maison Païenne (Pagan House) which was built in the twelfth century. It can be found before entering the town gate.

Inside the gate, on the right, stands a superb edifice, the church of St Pierre et St Paul. Together with that of Marmoutier, this represents among the most outstanding Romanesque art in Alsace. Beautifully restored in 1968, constructed of golden stone, it has walls decorated, as at Marmoutier, in the Lombard style, pierced by perfect rounded arches, rising to a later octagonal tower of red and yellow blocks of dressed stone. The simplicity and finesse of the work make a wonderful sight. At roof height, curious carvings can be seen: a cross-legged man, lions devouring men, lions crouching, and the apostles. Inside, more odd little figures can be seen on the capitals. The organ, restored, is a Silbermann of 1733.

The main street leaves the town through the archway of a large square clocktower. Beside it stands a big disused well with three pulleys.

BOERSCH
On D35, 33 km from Strasbourg and 617 km from Calais

Only 3 kilometres further, the road passes through another fortified gateway and climbs to the exquisite cobbled main square of the village of Boersch. In the square, in front of the *hôtel de ville*, is another grand old well. Its three stone pillars rise to a stone covering from which hang three pulleys and three buckets, all now full of flowers. A stream runs through the village in a channel, going underneath the *hôtel de ville*. From the *place*, the main street runs runs through the middle of the village, winding between attractive houses, until it leaves by the gateway at the far end.

ANDLAU
On D425, 35 km from Strasbourg and 624 km from Calais

Andlau village lies comfortably in the valley of the sprightly River Andlau, the slopes of its vine-covered hills rising on either side. High on the slope, its church can be seen, a slender pointed black spire poised on a pink octagonal stone tower. The streets of the village, its centre almost entirely cobbled, twist around between marvellously picturesque old houses. Some are particularly fine, with balconies or turrets as well as the usual generosity of carved timbers, shutters and flower boxes. There are small, appealing squares, like Place de l'Hôtel de Ville with its octagonal fountain.

Follow the river through the village – houses back on to the waterside – to reach the church, once part of a distinguished convent which existed here from the ninth century until the Revolution. The church survived, its high tower, with a balcony all around, dating from the seventeenth century. Much of the rest of the building is far older, being an excellent example of twelfth-century Romanesque. A great quantity of carving decorates the façade in an intriguing frieze of animals and men, real, legendary, mythical and allegorical. The Romanesque porch, too, is superb and contains good sculpture. Notice how the question of what form the biblical serpent took before being condemned to creep on the earth is dealt with: in the porch here he is shown upright, his head among the apples, one of which he offers to Eve.

The road to the church continues to climb beside the river, leaving the village and going into the hills, soon giving sight of the ruined châteaux of Spesbourg and Haut-Andlau, just two of several fortresses which protected this area. Higher still, the road reaches Le Hohwald, a mountain resort village with hotels and villas, ideally placed for some leisurely touring by car or on foot in the Alsace uplands.

A typical village house of Alsace

ITTERSWILLER
On D35 and D365, 37 km from Strasbourg and 626 km from Calais

Standing high on a ridge, with some wonderfully pretty old houses (and a number of new houses constructed quite successfully in the old style), this wine village is especially appealing for its marvellous views. On the approach from Andlau, the road reveals a magnificent vista across forested hills descending into the vine-filled valley. There are restaurants and hotels dotted along the main street as it descends through the village.

BLIENSCHWILLER
On D35, 40 km from Strasbourg and 661 km from Calais

From one village to the next along this part of the wine country can be as little as a few kilometres. Not all deserve a pause, though at each little place there are traditional cottages, and vine growers tend their fields to make traditional Alsace wines. Suspended on wires, immaculately kept, the neat rows of grapevines grow exceptionally tall. Tractors driving into the fields can be completely lost to view as they make their way up and down the rows.

From Itterswiller, the Wine Road presses on between vines, while beyond rise forested slopes. It comes to Nothalten, a working community that makes little provision for tourists, in effect, just a long street with a fountain at each end. Yet it, too, has a generous helping of charm.

A couple of kilometres further reaches Blienschwiller, another sweet, delightful, working village, but with many outstanding examples of picturesque traditional architecture.

The Alsace Vosges

The village square forms an open triangle with a large, octagonal fountain. As the main street winds through, it passes a succession of pretty old houses of jaunty, uneven shapes. Several have been painted gaudy colours. One has a green upper storey, orange first floor, and a stone base in mauve. Its next-door neighbour is bright red.

Yet this remains a typical working village with few tourists. Several local wine producers can be found here; many have attractive wrought-iron signs outside their premises.

DAMBACH-LA-VILLE
On D35, 40 km from Strasbourg and 661 km from Calais

A factory with its chimney provides the unpromising first glimpse of Dambach. Just before the road enters the walls of the fortified village, a sign on the right points up through the vines to a little lonely Romanesque chapel, St Sébastien, which gives a superb view over the surrounding country. Inside, the simple church has an unexpectedly ornate

Vineyards of Alsace as autumn approaches

seventeenth-century baroque altar.

Passing through Dambach's imposing *porte haute*, the through-road – taking a fair amount of traffic – skirts the village centre and rapidly leaves again through the big, stone tower of the eastern gate. Instead, turn up Rue du Général de Gaulle to discover the quiet, pleasing heart of the village. Some houses have been thoroughly modernized, others have kept all their old character.

Many have the traditional steep roofs, a multitude of angled timbers, bright shutters, exposed slabs of pink stone, and flowers in abundance. Large archways lead into attractive courtyards.

The delightful, peaceful village centre is Place du Marché, overlooked by the fine *hôtel de ville*, its stepped gable full of shuttered windows. Behind the square, the pink stone church represents a jumble of styles – it was rebuilt in 1862. Continue beyond the church to find the third gate of triangular Dambach. Rue des Ours leads back down from the square to the main road, passing several handsome houses. Many belong to wine growers from whom visitors can buy their product.

Leaving the village, you'll see a small and unusual estate of new housing: boxy, modern houses, but built at all angles and painted in gaudy 'traditional' colours, including purple!

CHÂTENOIS
On N59, 40 km from Strasbourg and 661k m from Calais

Approaching through the vines from Dambach and Scherwiller, cross over the busy N59 to reach the centre of Châtenois. Or, if you have come into Alsace passing beneath the Vosges mountains *par le tunnel* (as it is shown on the roadsigns), and emerging at Ste-Marie-aux-Mines on the N59, Châtenois will be the first Alsace wine village you reach – turn right off the main road to enter this big, busy village.

Many attractive old buildings in the traditional style give the village much appeal. There's an interesting, Romanesque belltower, and a fifteenth-century gateway, known as the Tour des Sorcières (witches' tower). Storks, which once were a common sight in Alsace and a symbol of

A peaceful place to rest

the region, nest on top. In the village centre there's an enticing Logis hotel, Le Dontenville.

KINTZHEIM
On D35, 42 km from Strasbourg and 663 km from Calais

Only 2 kilometres south of Châtenois, at Kintzheim, more lovely timbered houses can be seen along the main street, and another interesting tall church spire. Sideroads often present an even prettier array of cottages. Unusual attractions just outside the village include the Montagne des Singes, an open-air monkey reserve, and the Volerie des Aigles, where trained birds of prey perform in the open courtyard of a ruined fourteenth-century castle. Both are just off D159.

From here, D159 climbs further to the magnificent castle of Haut-Koenigsbourg (see St-Hippolyte, below). Either reach the Haut-Koenigsbourg castle from Kintzheim and descend on the steep winding road to St-Hippolyte, or, leaving the castle for a moment, continue southward on the Wine Road, D35. The road passes through Orschwiller, a former possession of Haut-Koenigsbourg, lying directly

Opposite:
Ripe and ready

below the fortress. Perhaps not quite so striking as its neighbours, yet here, too, are some delightful houses, and vineyards reaching right into the village centre.

Volerie des Aigles open daily April–Sept. p.m. only; Sept.–Nov. p.m. only on Wed., Sat., Sun. and fêtes. Montagne des Singes open daily April–Sept.; Sept.– Nov. on Wed., Sat., Sun. and fêtes

ST-HIPPOLYTE
On D1B, 46 km from Strasbourg and 667 km from Calais

An especially delightful village of flowers and fountains, little squares and marvellous old timbered cottages, St-Hippolyte forms a neat square. In effect, it is fortified by the outer houses which seem to make a protective wall around the others. Turrets at its corners enhance the village defenses, and a channel of water at the periphery could pass for a simple moat.

Within the village, some houses have become skewwhiff with age (or were they built like that?), and many have magnificent timberwork and ornamental stonework. There are many carved lintels of wood or stone, and a few have complete window frames of carved stone, an attractive reddish colour. Corner timbers, too, are often ornately carved. So faithful is the village to its local style that even new, modern lintels have been carved and decorated. Courtyards and and busy, open-fronted wine cellars give further appeal – St-Hippolyte produces a good red wine, something unusual in Alsace.

Water flows not just round the village, but beneath it, emerging from outlets within a succession of decorative fountains. In Rue des Cigognes and Rue St Fulrade are fine examples. Wander in the backstreets to find more attractive old houses and more fountains. From the main street, Route du Vin, the castle of Haut-Koenigsbourg can be seen high on a hill. The parish church rises to a bulbous dome, while at the southern edge of the village there's a mauve-painted chapel – the private property of an old people's home – just on the corner of the Haut-Koenigsbourg turning.

This steep lane winds and climbs some 6 kilometres to the imposing medieval fortress, which dominates a vast panorama of the blue Vosges hills and the Rhine valley. A massive structure occupying the irregular, craggy summit of a wooded peak, the castle makes a thrilling sight. A feudal château dating originally from the early twelfth century, much enlarged in 1480, it fell into ruin in the seventeenth and eighteenth centuries. In 1901, during the hated period of German rule, it was given to the Kaiser, Wilhelm II, by the city of Sélestat which was responsible for its upkeep. He then had the castle restored superbly, though with only fanciful adherence to the original appearance. Nonetheless, it has become one of the most impressive sights in Alsace, recognisable to anyone who saw Renoir's film *La Grande Illusion*, for which it formed a backdrop.

Outer ramparts enclose an inner fortress with a massive, high keep and seigneurial apartments. Interiors are furnished as if by Hollywood, with massive wooden tables, suits of armour, medieval weapons and crests and pennants and huge antlered hunting trophies.

St-Hippolyte, an especially delightful village

Château de Haut-Koenigsbourg open daily except fêtes; closed Jan.

BERGHEIM

On D1B, 50 km from Strasbourg and 671 km from Calais

The Wine Road continues through a coloured quilt of vineyards to reach another village protected by its outer wall of houses. At Bergheim, though, the defensive intent is more obvious, because to enter the village you must pass through an impressive medieval fortified gateway. Before it comes a first rampart of houses, then a moat, now cultivated as gardens. Then the imposing *porte haute* is reached. Dated 1300, and with a gilded clock, the gate is within a mighty tower of stone, beneath a roof of glazed, coloured tiles arranged in crisscross pattern.

The main street runs straight through the village from the gateway. On both sides, and even more so down the sidestreets, stand some attractive old houses, several with delightful courtyards. The same reddish stone, in fine, rounded blocks, is exposed on the corners of the houses and on the lintels over doors and windows. Outside houses, cut timber has been stacked for use in the hearth.

The principal square, cobbled Place du Marché with its octagonal fountain, opens out in front of the pink stone *hôtel*

Fortified Bergheim

de ville. Rue du Haut-Koenigsbourg, leading off, is tremendously pretty, with overhanging timbered houses swathed in geraniums and other flowers. Along the north side of the village can be seen another vestige of ancient fortifications, a rampart with three towers.

HUNAWIHR

On D1B, 55 km from Strasbourg and 676 km from Calais

The rustic character of the Wine Road is briefly interrupted by the town of Ribeauvillé, itself with a fair helping of Alsatian charm and plenty to see. Three ruined castles stand together above the town – the large château of St Ulrich, smaller Girsberg above it, and higher still, the simpler lookout of Haut-Ribeaupierre.

Painted houses and rich vineyards

Continue past Ribeauvillé and turn right on to the road into Hunawihr. Before entering the village, glance up at the hills: from here the three ruined châteaux can be seen even more clearly. Hunawihr makes an attractive cluster of

Hunawihr's fortified church

typical twisted old stone-and-timber, wattle and daub cottages climbing a hillside, with vines coming into the heart of the village. A single street winds through, with cobbled yards set back, surrounded by more houses.

Bright flowers grow everywhere and the houses too are bright, sometimes even gaudy, with painted exteriors. Some have unlikely colours – green, pink, orange, mauve, even a pillar-box red – and often of a startling, Disney-like brilliance giving the impression of a place which is hardly real.

At the centre, where the *mairie* stands facing a fountain, a sideroad leads up towards Hunawihr's handsome church. From in front of the building there's a magnificent view over the vines towards wooded crests on the far side. Although the village is not fortified or defended, its church does have a fortress-like quality. It stands within grounds enclosed by a high wall forming an octagon, entered through a sturdy arched gateway with a tower. Instead of the typical bulbous black spire, the belfry is big, solid, square, and looks like a castle keep.

Inside, the church is all of the local pink-tinted stone. A large wooden gallery and organ loft cuts across a simple Gothic interior. Beneath the tower, a small room with an elaborately vaulted ceiling retains fifteenth-century murals. A massive iron bell displayed in here, carved and decorated, was cast in 1700 and is called 'Huna'. Another oddity about the church: it serves both Protestant and Catholic villagers.

Between Hunawihr and the main road, the Parc des Cigognes combines being an attraction for visitors with a serious breeding programme to assist with the reintroduction of storks into Alsace. To help with the former role, in addition to storks it keeps numerous other water birds. Storks used to be characteristic of Alsace, but overhunting in Africa (to which they migrate), together with loss of habitat in Alsace, led to a catastrophic decline in their numbers. Now a concerted effort is being made to save the Alsace storks from extinction.

Parc des Cigognes (Stork Park) open daily April–Sept. a.m. and p.m.; Oct.–11 Nov. on Wed., Sat., Sun. and fêtes only

RIQUEWIHR
On D3, off D1B, 58 km from Strasbourg and 679 km from Calais

By great good fortune, ancient Riquewihr, respected for centuries for its Riesling wines, completely escaped damage during the Second World War while many of its nearest neighbours suffered. It also happened to be one of the loveliest, most delightful gems of Alsace charm and tradition. Today, it remains a working, wine-making village; only great tourist popularity has slightly diminished its appeal.

The old centre – almost the whole village – is enclosed within a rampart of houses which turn their backs to the outside world. Arched gateways give entrance to this simple fortress which rises up a gentle slope. However, only residents may drive in the village; all other vehicles must be left at pay car parks around the perimeter. On the southeast corner, defensive walls survive from the fortifications of Riquewihr's château. Inside the village, a festive air prevails for much of the year, especially in October. A jolly *petit train touristique* takes visitors on a jaunt up and down the hill. In autumn, when the new wine has been pressed and is sold from street stalls, there's a veritable party feeling along the cobbled main street, Rue du Général de Gaulle, and the little courtyards and squares which lie on either side. Often local uniformed brass bands play in the streets.

At the lower end, the main gate comes through the *hôtel de ville*. First turning on the left, Cour du Château, leads to the sixteenth-century château. The building, with a slender tower, now houses a history of the Alsatian Post Office.

The main street continues past the old communal oven, dated 1602, now a boutique. A succession of shops and stalls sell local produce from vineyards and farms, especially traditional sausages and smoked meats. All the way up the street, there are marvellous old buildings, fountains and pretty squares. Some houses have fortifications, and most buildings are entered through an archway in pink stone, often decoratively carved. Restaurant L'Écurie occupies a cobbled courtyard within wooden gates. Rue des Trois Églises on the right leads into a delightful, small square dominated by the village's principal place of worship, a large Protestant church, plain and austere in the evangelical style.

The main street rises at last to the extraordinary Dolder, a sturdy tower-gateway of pink-tinted stone, with an elaborate, wood-framed upper section containing dwellings, and an old clock set into the wall. Right at the top is the bell whose chimes add to the character of this upper part of the village. Built in 1291, reinforced in the fifteenth and sixteenth centuries, the Dolder now houses a museum of local history

*Riquewihr at dusk –
no filter was used to
take this photograph*

and archaeology. From the top, it gives superb views over the surrounding country.

Narrow Rue des Juifs, beside the Dolder on the right, leads into Cour des Juifs, a small square with its sixteenth-century fountain. The street and square were once a densely occupied Jewish ghetto, proof enough that Riquewihr has had a long and successful history. Every town of note in Alsace had its Jewish quarter at one time. (Captain Dreyfus, the army captain imprisoned on trumped-up charges in the notorious anti-Semitic 'Affair', was from Alsace). During Germany's Nazi era, many Jewish families at first fled into Alsace, only to be rounded up there by the invading German troops. Now German tourists stroll in the tiny ghetto. Also in the Cour: a staircase leads up to a section of town wall with a curious tower, the Tour des Voleurs, formerly a prison and torture chamber now open as a morbid tourist attraction.

Pass through the Dolder and you have not quite left the village enclosure. There is a second ring of defenses, formed by houses, penetrated by the *obertor* or upper gate. This massive stone structure dates from 1400 and preserves an impressive portcullis and drawbridge together with the wooden contraption for operating them, which is still in working order.

Riquewihr's main street rises to the medieval Dolder

Despite its popularity, getting away from tourists presents no great problem at Riquewihr. Almost all the visitors simply troop up and down the main street. Sidestreets and even tinier alleys in between, cobbled and full of character, have just as much appeal. Many of the houses along back roads are magnificent, with arches behind arches, and often draped with greenery. Rue de la Première Armée, Rue de Strasbourg, Rue Dintzheim, for example, reward a leisurely stroll.

Post Office Museum open April–Nov. a.m. and p.m. closed Tue.

KIENTZHEIM
On D1B, 63 km from Strasbourg and 684 km from Calais

The Wine Road travels from Riquewihr through and near villages that sustained considerable war damage. Bennwihr, completely destroyed, has been rebuilt and is a pleasant modern *village fleuri* (i.e. it is listed as one of France's 'flowery villages'), still noted for fine wine. It has a striking new church, the interior resembling a conference hall with a wall of vivid modern stained glass.

One kilometre after Bennwihr, the Wine Road takes a right turn to reach Sigolsheim, also badly damaged, and ancient Kientzheim, much of which luckily managed to survive.

Defensively laid out all in a square, with ramparts in places, Kientzheim is entered through a fine arched gateway with a little medieval château beside it. Both the gateway, called Porte du Lalli, and the château, like much else in the village, were transformed in the sixteenth century. Today, the Confrèrie St Étienne, which oversees the quality of Alsace wines, has its headquarters in the château, while the Lalli gateway houses a museum of the region's wine and vineyards.

Beside Porte du Lalli, a splendid sixteenth-century cobbled courtyard can be seen in the Ancien Cour des Chevaliers de Malte (Court of the Knights of Malta), now the private property of a wine grower. Close by, a pretty *place* has restaurant tables laid out beside an elaborate covered well of pink stone, now bursting with flowers.

The backstreets, too, provide pleasing corners to discover. In the village church, with its restored Gothic tower, good statuary and stonework can be found.

At the upper end of the village, towers mark the corners of the ramparts. The *porte haute* itself, though, has disappeared, demolished in 1875. Standing outside the walls just here, a French tank stands in reminder of the hard struggle in 1944–45 to free this part of Alsace from German occupation.

Wine museum open daily June–Oct. a.m. and p.m.

KAYSERSBERG
On D28, 65 km from Strasbourg and 686 km from Calais

Woodland replaces vineyards as the road climbs a mile further into satisfying old Kaysersberg. Hills rise up steeply all around. While in most villages of the Alsace Wine Road, pale green grapevines can be seen growing just beyond the end of the main street, here forest grows at the edge of the village. For all that, the vines of Kaysersberg produce a noted wine. On a hill behind, a round fortress tower, remnant of a château, stands watchfully.

Although a pleasingly irregular shape, roughly following first the right bank and then the left of the River Weiss, the whole place had ramparts all around. Of these, some good stretches of wall and four sturdy, round towers remain in various states of repair. A pair of storks are in residence on the pointed turret of one of the towers, Tour Kessler Turm, their nest looking like a precariously balanced, battered fur hat.

A long main street, Rue du Général de Gaulle or Grand' Rue, meanders delightfully through from one end of the village to the other. It's heavily cobbled, as are sidestreets, and while locals tear through with admirable lack of concern for their tyres, by far the best way to get around is to park and stroll. Even on foot, though, the cobbles can be hard going. Fortunately, several well-placed bars and restaurants make it easy and enjoyable to take a break.

The name of this ancient village refers not to the German kaiser but to Caesar. Originally this site – fortified ever since – marked an important Roman guardpost between Gaul and the Rhine. However, in 1226 it did become a possession of a kaiser, Frederick II, who purchased the castle for ready money. The village and its inhabitants came as part of the deal. He built the defenses, and in 1296 the community became an independent and privileged free town, prospering for centuries from its distinguished Tokay wines.

Rue du Général de Gaulle passes a succession of extremely attractive Renaissance and older houses, mansions and civic buildings, as well as ornate Renaissance fountains, and tubs of flowers. Walking up from the lower end of the village, the imposing *hôtel de ville* in local Renaissance style soon appears on the right. Beside it, the church dates from the twelfth to fifteenth centuries and combines good work from across the centuries, including a Romanesque portal with curious, naive carvings of real and mythical creatures. Inside the building, much excellent sculpture of the sixteenth century can be seen. A huge, agonized Christ, realistically bleeding, hangs above the nave. A cobbled alley

Kaysersberg nestles amid wooded hills

Opposite:
*The stone bridge
at the heart of
Kaysersberg, and
the ruined fortress
above the village*

winds around the church, giving access to a small cemetery in which lie the men who died liberating the little town from Nazi rule.

The road makes a gentle curve, passing on the left a local history and archaeology museum located in superb, Renaissance premises within a magnificent courtyard. Soon after, the road turns again to cross the cobbled, fortified little stone bridge over the River Weiss. The bridge, with lovely sixteenth-century houses on each side, the river frothing fast over big boulders, makes an exceptionally enjoyable pause. In the middle of the bridge, a shrine shelters a peculiar stone Madonna and Child. From here the château on the hill makes a dramatic sight, its long stone wall and rounded tower rising above the rooftops. Rue des Forgerons, a turning in front of Maison du Forgeron (which contains an art gallery), leads up to the ruins: it takes about fifteen minutes on foot.

Beyond the bridge, the charming Renaissance architecture continues to delight. At the top of the cobbled main street, the very last house in the village was the birthplace of Albert Schweitzer (1875–1965), the remarkable doctor (and poet, musician, priest ...) who won the Nobel Peace Prize in 1952. The house itself, handsomely colonnaded, makes a striking impression. It now contains the Dr Schweitzer Cultural Centre and Museum. Part of the Schweitzer home is a tiny Protestant church. Just outside the enclosure of the ancient village, an old stone tower and a bust of Schweitzer stand in public gardens.

Dr Schweitzer Museum open May–Oct. a.m. and p.m., also open Easter. Municipal museum open Easter to end Oct. a.m. and p.m. on Sun. and fêtes only; except July–Aug. when open daily a.m. and p.m.

NIEDERMORSCHWIHR
On D11ii, 67 km from Strasbourg and 688 km from Calais

The road runs through steep, turning hills, some covered with vines, some with trees, to reach this pleasing wine village. It consists of hardly more than a single street, almost completely lined with picturesque traditional old houses and punctuated with disused stone wells and

The Villages of Northern France

Niedermorschwihr has remarkably pretty corners

fountains. Many buildings have fine wrought-iron signs hanging outside.

Everything here seems to have a slightly uneven look! The handful of crooked backstreets make oddly-shaped corners on which oddly-shaped cottages have been built to fit. The plain and simple church, too, just behind the main street, has a twisted spire.

Of the few sidestreets, Rue des Vignerons, Rue Ribeaupierre and Rue des Trois Épis create a little *place* in front of the *hôtel de ville* near the top of the village. Look down Rue Ribeaupierre for a startling example of the bright, colourful exteriors that Alsatians often like. Three houses together, by an old stone well full of flowers, have been given a comic book allure in dazzling orange, blue, and red.

There's more twisting and turning on the mountain road up to Les Trois Épis. It gives great views much of the way, as does the shorter, but equally serpentine lane which cuts through tall vines towards Turckheim.

TURCKHEIM
On D10, 67 km from Strasbourg and 688 km from Calais

First impressions can be deceptive. Despite being a moderately sized town rather than a village, with a screeching railway line passing through, and smoking factory chimneys around the edges, Turckheim abudantly rewards a visit.

The town lies on the left bank of the River Fecht, and its vineyards have long been acclaimed for the white Le Brand wine. Step through the archway of its sturdy, square fourteenth-century Porte de France – the gateway of pink stone and timber leading to the fortified, old town centre – and the scene becomes unrecognizably transformed. Just within the gateway (atop which perches a nesting basket for storks) lies Place Turenne, a handsome cobbled square. Here a traditional octagonal fountain almost blocks the entrance of the large sixteenth-century stone building of D'Wacht (the local Corps de Garde or gendarmerie), which now also houses the tourist office.

Leading off, Rothsgasse penetrates the old town, passing between numerous picturesque old dwellings, almost all dating from the Renaissance, magnificent old houses with overhanging upper stories of timber. A distinctive feature of many houses is the projecting upper room, enclosed balcony or covered gallery, often supported by one or two pillars. Rothsgasse comes at once to a square in front of the *hôtel de ville* and the Hôtel des Deux Clefs – the former is the town hall, the latter an appealing 2-star hotel of fine stone and timberwork, and with a large old-fashioned wrought-iron sign hanging over the street, dated 1620. Just beyond, a church in pink stone has a high steep slender spire of green, blue and yellow decorated tiles.

Everywhere, as in other villages along the Wine Road, disused stone wells have been prettified with flowers, a pulley wheel still hanging from the stone crosspiece. Almost every street or alley seems to have some interest. Rothsgasse (also known as Rue du Conseil) reaches Rue des Vignerons. To the right, this leads to another town gate, Porte du Brand. Left, it runs to the third gate of the triangular town, Porte de Munster.

Between Porte de Munster and Place Turenne extends the main street of the fortified village, Grand' Rue. Cobbled, lined on both sides with lovely old houses, this is dramatically beautiful. Look behind the dwellings to see steeply sloped vineyards coming down. Most buildings along the street have become business premises, with ornate wrought-iron signs hanging outside. Either side of Grand' Rue are marvellous cobbled courtyards. Number 3, for example, leads through an archway into Cour des

Cigognes. Number 37 has remarkable timberwork. Number 34, opposite, is within a delightful courtyard. Number 42 has a fine example of an overhanging storey supported by stone pillars, while number 47 has another, unsupported and seeming to defy gravity. On many houses the exposed cornerstones are large, pink wedges of rock. Often a single, huge piece of pink stone serves as a door frame, window frame or lintel. Along the street, several good hotels and restaurants invite a long pause.

A tiny cottage tucked into a corner of Turckheim's ancient Porte de France gateway

FRENCH FLANDERS

The very name of Flanders echoes with greatness. Throughout the Middle Ages, it represented prosperity, learning and high culture, a style of painting, of weaving, of architecture, a land whose craftsmen and artists were in demand throughout western Europe. That domain has long gone, divided between France, Belgium and the Netherlands. Yet the land is still there, so are its people, their language, traditions and memories.

A drive across these wide landscapes under big skies is like a journey across the pages of history. The story of western Europe has been carved into these fields, which have seen battles not just during this century but throughout the ages. There are more British military cemeteries in Flanders than anywhere else.

There's far more to Flanders, though, than its past. Today this is a vital, dynamic region of enterprise and industry, commerce and communications. As the large-scale manufacturing and mining of the past have seen a decline, new economic activities have sprung up. Lille, the capital of French Flanders, looks set fair to become a major European crossroads of trade and travel in the next century. TGVs connect it to Calais and Paris, and the new city-centre railway station, Lille-Europe, receives the Eurostar high-speed rail services which link it rapidly with Brussels and, through the Channel Tunnel, with London.

In the midst of all this, Flanders retains many rural corners, farming villages and little market towns of character. Their distinctive, Flemish qualities are simple low houses of brick and lofty ornate civic belfries, spacious paved main squares, tall steep-roofed Renaissance mansions with elaborate gables, large churches with meeeting-hall interiors, and in several places, festivals where the Giants come on parade to lead the whole town in procession.

These *fêtes des géants* have obscure origins; the Giants are huge models of people, male or female, usually in medieval dress, sometimes real historical figures, sometimes allegorical characters representing the local man or woman. Some towns and villages have one Giant, some have a whole family of them. They have names, and are regarded with affection by the local people, for whom they act as a curious kind of figurehead. Tourist offices can tell you if the village has a Giant, and when he or she will make an appearance.

Originally, Flanders came into being as a Roman colony, called Belgium after its native inhabitants, the Belgae. When Rome fell, Franks moved in, so Flanders in the fifth century had already begun sharing its history with that of France. It became part of Charlemagne's empire, and in 843, by the Treaty of Verdun, passed to his grandson Charles II who, in turn, granted it to his son-in-law

Baudouin. Under Baudouin and his descendants, Flanders became a vast, independent county, and achieved exceptional prosperity from trade and cloth manufacturing. However, flat and hard to defend, it was an unstable political entity much threatened by its neighbours.

It became a possession of the Dukes of Burgundy in 1385. Many Flemish craftsmen moved south to the rich duchy, taking skills and customs which now are more often thought of as typically Burgundian, such as patterned roofs of glazed, coloured tiles. In 1477, by inheritance, Flanders came into the domain of the Hapsburgs, the powerful Austrian dynasty who were also kings of Spain and had possessions all over Europe.

The stepped gable so typical of Flanders

So it was that Charles I of Spain, becoming Emperor Charles V, inherited an immense area of Europe. His attempts to rule and control his empire failed as he fought on several fronts to prevent its disintegration. One of his problems was France, with whom he waged war for over twenty years. In the process, he lost much of Flanders, and his son Philippe II lost more. As the Empire broke up, Flanders became one of Austria's possessions. But the French continued to eat into southern Flanders, taking it piece by piece. Its southern cities became French during the seventeenth century. Vauban, the great military architect of that time, put in place a magnificent system of defences clear across the Flemish territories France had won. Many northern towns still have his superb fortifications.

In 1790, a year after the French Revolution, French Flanders was formally annexed as the Nord département. That was certainly not the end of the story, though. The Austrians continued to fight back, besieging Lille in 1792. Some of the region indeed slipped out of French control altogether (Ypres, for example) but for the most part the French grip did not weaken. It has remained in France to this day.

However, many of its inhabitants, especially in urban areas, rightly consider themselves as much Flemish as French. They have a Franco-Flemish patois of their own, and many of their towns and villages keep Flemish names and a Flemish atmosphere.

Dunkerque – the dune church – is one of them. Although a major industrial port, backed by a vast area of oil refineries and chemical works, a likeable Flemish provincial town survives at the middle. The town hall in Place Valentin is typically ornate in the Flemish style. For many Britons, Dunkerque is synonymous with the evacuation of Allied forces in 1940, when between 25 May and 4 June, 350,000 men escaped from the town's old port as the Germans advanced. Somehow, this has gone into British folk history as a sort of victory. The whole story is told in Dunkerque's museum – from the French point of view.

Just inland from the Channel, St-Omer is another interesting Flemish town. Its pleasant town centre has many attractive, historic mansions. In the large central square, the museum in Hôtel Sandelin displays a good collection of medieval Flemish art and crafts. The immense Gothic basilica of Notre Dame rises above the town.

Arras, a border town on the southern limits of Flanders, has always suffered badly from war. Tall, steeply gabled Flemish mansions line its two magnificent arcaded central squares – huge Grande Place and little Place des Heros. The exquisite sixteenth-century town hall, completely destroyed during the last war, has been faithfully rebuilt. Inside it can be found the entrance to an extraordinary system of underground passageways which for a thousand years have provided the citizens of Arras with shelter during wartime.

Memorials, military cemeteries and battle sites surround the town. Eight kilometres away, the Great War battlefield of Vimy Ridge has been preserved just as it was.

Lille, the region's capital, lies at the heart of one of Europe's major industrial areas. Yet it has a bustling, pleasant old quarter with many impressive buildings, old and new. Stroll the narrow backstreets of Le Vieux Lille, and wander in the lively town centre boulevards and squares, to find the twelfth-century Hospice Comtesse; the huge, seventeenth-century Porte de Paris; Vauban's impressive and powerful *citadelle*; and some astonishingly elaborate Flemish baroque buildings like the seventeenth-century Ancienne Bourse, the fifteenth-century Palais Rihour, and in the same tradition, the nineteenth-century Théâtre de l'Opéra, which has statues emerging from the walls. The city's Musée Beaux-Arts (Fine Arts Museum), in Place de la République, holds a renowned collection of Flemish and northern French painters. It's a lively city of entertainment and good living, and several of Lille's restaurants have won acclaim among the French food guides.

Flemish cooking has kept its own style, combining with French influences to create a rich, hearty cuisine of strong flavours. Substantial stews are the great speciality, especially *hochepot*, a thick meat and vegetable hotpot. *Charcuterie*, sausages and *andouillettes*, tripe and spicy *pâtés* are all popular. Beer – a great deal of it being brewed locally – finds its way into several

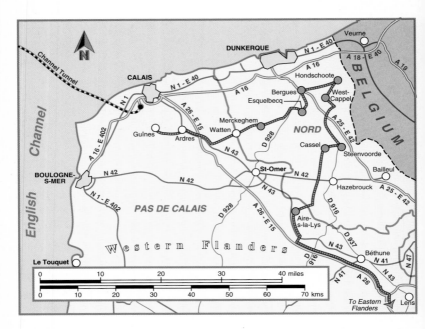

dishes; *carbonade flamande*, featured on many menus, is beef braised with beer.

Cheese plays a big part at the Flemish table, though some varieties are so strong that even locals consider it a joke. There is said to be a kind of cheese which may not be carried on public transport in Lille. Pungent smelling, but not quite so strong tasting, the Flemish cheeses are of the soft and creamy, washed-rind variety, often sold in a wooden box. Not only cheese on its own, but cheese pastries, cheese flans and tarts are much liked. Everywhere in Flanders (but especially near Maroilles, in the eastern part of the region), bakeries and restaurants offer *flamiche au Maroilles*, a tart of Maroilles cheese. Bakery items generally feature strongly. Waffles and pancakes, as well, make a frequent appearance in either sweet or savoury mode. Whole meals can be eaten of them.

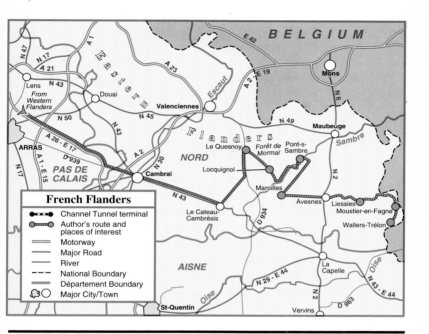

French Flanders

●━━● Channel Tunnel terminal

○━━○ Author's route and places of interest

═══ Motorway

─── Major Road

─── River

─ ─ ─ National Boundary

· · · Département Boundary

✿○ Major City/Town

MERCKEGHEM
On D226, 42 km (via N43) southeast of Calais

From the Channel Tunnel, there is no need to travel into Calais merely to leave the town again. The Calais Terminal stands on the doorstep of the region, and country lanes lead away from it directly into the Flanders plain. Head first for Guînes on the D231 (via junction 11 of *autoroute* A16), and from there to Ardres. Between the two villages, a simple stone monument records in gilt letters the exact location of the Field of the Cloth of Gold, where in 1520 Henry VIII of England and François I of France met in rival splendour to discuss the irritating matter of England's title to this whole region of France. The encounter turned instead into a battle of ostentation, each side trying to appear the more stately, wealthy and regal, and with the greater reason to disdain the other. It's now a field of cabbages. Ardres has an excellent village hotel and restaurant, the Grand Hôtel Clément.

From Ardres, travel on N43 or on quieter back lanes to

Watten, a little town with quaysides busy with barges at the meeting of the River Aa and the Canal de la Haute Colme. The Tunnel-Paris high-speed railway line carrying Eurostar trains passes close by. The D226 rises from Watten, a narrow, rustic lane. Crossing the railway line, it climbs along a ridge which marks the inland edge of the watery flat plain of maritime Flanders.

Here, at least, Flanders becomes hilly farm country, bucolic and intimate, and the road reaches Merckeghem, a tiny village on the heights. There's little more here than a single street of plain, brick houses, many of them single-storey, and a yellow brick church. Fields of pasture press against the dwellings.

The village street follows the line of the crest of the hill, and gives a magnificent, fascinating view of the coastal plain. It seems to stand far aloof from all the intense human activity below, the mixture of the simplest agriculture and the heaviest industry. Great and little waterways run across the land. Villages and steeples and factory chimneys extend to the sea – Dunkerque can be seen on the horizon. The silence of the air, gazing on such a vast, historic landscape of energy and endeavour, of peace and war, has an almost eerie quality.

ESQUELBECQ
On D17, 20 km south of Dunkerque and 51 km from Calais

In the midst of flat, arable fields, this quiet village preserves a strong flavour of old Flanders. Around its paved little central square, Grand' Place, the neat low frontages come in all the hues that brick can be. Flower boxes at the windows make a pretty decoration. Brick again, this time in crisscrossed red and cream shades, was used to make the large church in the square. It dates from the sixteenth century and inside has the 'meeting hall' style of the region, but divided into three naves.

What would otherwise be a typical Flemish village gains an unexpected air of dignity by having a grand château in its own park. This, too, is made entirely of brick, with big, round corner towers and enclosed by a moat. It remained almost unaltered since being completed in 1610. Then in 1984 part of this fine edifice collapsed: the repair work continues.

Opposite:
Crisscross patterns in the church brickwork

BERGUES
On D916, 10 km from Dunkerque and 55 km from Calais

One of the most precious jewels of western Flanders, the irregularly shaped walled centre of the little fortress town of Bergues has been brilliantly restored following wartime damage. Where new building has taken the place of old, the meeting of ancient and modern has been achieved with style and feeling, keeping always within the bounds of Flemish tradition. The town feels comfortable with its long history. In June and December, colourful festivals fill the streets, under the lofty eye of the black-suited and top-hatted local *géant*.

Follow signs for Bergues-Centre: the road narrows to cross a moat and a drawbridge, and passes through a gateway in the mighty earth-banked brick ramparts. Within the walls, attractive squares and streets interweave erratically, always lined with brick cottages and tall town houses under steep roofs, high gables and dormer windows. At one side of Place de la République, the largest square and the very heart of the town, a fortified yellow brick belfry rises from the arches of a covered market – a completely new structure faithfully replacing the sixteenth-

Canals form part of Bergues' defences

century belfry dynamited by the Germans in 1944. It houses a carillon which chimes every fifteen minutes, and at 5 p.m. on most summer days plays a short concert. On the strange black roof, reminiscent of a helmet, a Lion of Flanders sits 54 metres above the ground. At the foot of the belfry, the tourist office gives out useful leaflets about the town, once a leading producer of the woollen cloth for which Flanders was famed. Now it's in butter and cheese that Bergues excels.

From the tourist office a little *train touristique* starts a half-hour 4-kilometre tour within the fortifications. It passes by the various squares, each representing a different market that was held here – Marché au Fromage, Marché au Poisson, Marché aux Bestiaux, Marché aux Chevaux, Marché aux Volailles, and others – and circuits the magnificent walls with their solid towers, bastions and gateways. If you would prefer to walk, blue arrows mark a route around the town taking just under two hours.

The main shopping street, Rue Nationale, leads off the square, and continues round into Rue Faidherbe and Rue Carnot – along which some fine eighteenth-century houses survive, many with sculpted keystones over doors and windows – the three roads forming a circle which returns to Place de la République. Through the middle of this circle runs prosaically named Rue de la Gare, which passes Église St Martin. A large Gothic brick structure, this partly survived wartime bombing, and is partly new, the later section standing beside the ruined, older walls. A plain, fortified belfry stands separate from the rest of the church. In front, the war memorial, with its long lists of names and statue of a soldier riddled with holes, creates a powerful effect.

On a corner across from the church, the brick and pale stone Mont de Piété building, in decorative but elegant Renaissance style, seems to have survived relatively unharmed since the date over its doorway, 1630. Today there's a museum inside, with a mixed assortment of displays ranging from butterflies to medieval Flemish paintings.

Across Place de la République, facing the *Beffroi*, the seventeenth-century *hôtel de ville* has a rather over-elaborate dignity. Behind it, Rue du Gouvernement forms another little *place*, which leads the way to extensive public gardens. Here trees and wide gravelled paths occupy the site of the eleventh-century Benedictine Abbey which lay at the foundation of the town. A wider path climbs to a great stone octagonal block of a structure, looking like something made

of childrens' stacking bricks, facing another, round and pointed. The towers are all that remain of the abbey church. The hillock itself is Le Groenberg, the very origin of Bergues, the place on which St Winoc made his home in the seventh century.

Outside the walls, a confusing array of canals and streams provides additional defence for this brilliantly fortified little town. One of the waterways is the navigable Canal de Bergues, linking the town to the sea.

Museum open daily a.m. and p.m., excluding Tue. and Jan.

The lofty belfry rises above Bergues' town centre

HONDSCHOOTE
On D947, 22 km southeast of Dunkerque and 61 km from Calais

Looking out over a completely flat landscape, and with a well-preserved windmill on its outskirts, bright, quietly bustling Hondschoote is very much the small Flemish country town of today. Indeed, it is reputed as a Flemish-speaking centre, although in reality even here these days most people speak only French. During and after the Middle Ages, the great era of Flemish civilization and art, the town's population was ten times what it is now. It produced huge quantities of fine cloth: once, there were over 3,000 workshops in Hondschoote.

Not much remains of those times, and many of the buildings are postwar, although the traditional Flemish style

has been preserved. Then as now, the heart of Hondschoote was its spacious Grand' Place. In the middle of the square a bandstand, modern fountain and old willow tree stand together in a delightful little public garden, and a monument records the Victory of Hondschoote in 1793, when French forces defeated the Austrians, and their English allies.

Beside them, the yellow brick church, in late Gothic style and draped in part with leafy Virginia creeper, has impressive proportions hinting at the little town's erstwhile importance. Its immense sixteenth-century belfry, 82 metres tall, adorned with gargoyles, soars far above the rooftops and can be seen for miles.

Hondschoote's sixteenth-century town hall

Inside, despite some baroque decoration, the church has the uncomplicated Flemish look.

Around the rest of the *place*, newer buildings in red brick have kept the steep roof lines. Just a few are much older. Opposite the church, now the Caisse d'Epargne savings bank, stands the former manor of the Coppens, Hondschoote's local lords. More striking, along the side of the Grand' Place, the *hôtel de ville* (town hall) is an outstanding example of Flemish Renaissance civic architecture, dating from 1558. Made of stone instead of brick, attractive with flower boxes at the windows and ancient crests set into the wall, the façade is elaborate and decorative; a panel records more details of the Battle of

Opposite:
On the edge of town:
a windmill in the
flat fields of
Flanders

Hondschoote. A steep slate roof rises to a pointed belfry. Next door, well placed in the centre of town, the Auberge de l'Hôtel de Ville dates from 1617.

Town hall open to visits a.m. and p.m. during office working hours. Noord–Meulen windmill open daily for guided visits by a local resident

WEST-CAPPEL
On D4, 17 km south of Dunkerque and 60 km from Calais

Surrounded by absolutely flat fields of ploughed earth, this lonely village is, new and old houses alike, made of red brick under red tile roofs. The only exception is the large church at its centre – and that is in yellow brick. The Église St Sylvestre was rebuilt in the sixteenth century using this distinctive 'sand brick'. Inside, the brickwork is painted a functional white, and the three naves are separated by sturdy, round columns also in brick.

The church graveyard seems particularly full, but perhaps because a large proportion of the stones are for people who are still alive! Not just spouses, but sometimes both husband and wife are still alive yet have tombs ready and waiting. In one small section of the graveyard, in neat rows behind the church, British War Graves lie packed together.

They number sixty-nine in all, young men who died in the last stages of the withdrawal to Dunkerque. Most are simply 'A Soldier of the War 1939–1945'. Some have dates but no name, but a few have names with their ages. Sometimes the regiment is known. A few are 'buried near this spot'. The British military graves are enclosed by a clipped hedge; their corner of the cemetery is kept, as always, in immaculate condition by the Commonwealth War Graves Commission. A plaque, with a map, gives a full account of the war in Flanders in 1939 and 1940, showing the extent of the German victory at that stage.

Across the road from the church, the château is another substantial edifice in brick. It stands surrounded by a moat, within wooded grounds, in this flat, defenceless terrain on the Belgian border.

STEENVOORDE
On D947, 45 km from Dunkerque and 60 km from Calais

Windmills in a good state of preservation stand on the south and west of this likeable, workaday small town of simple Flemish-style brick houses under steep roofs. One mill is cylindrical and brick, the other square and wooden. Steenvoorde has a quiet, bustling air. Once famous for its great tapestries, now the little town is better known for dairy produce. Its imposing church with a tall spire is made all of yellow brick, yet makes an attempt at the flamboyant Gothic style. There's a big local festival here at the beginning of October, the Fête du Houblon (Hop Festival), when the *géant* Yan de Houtkapper emerges for his annual parade around town. The legend is that this local hero was the woodman who measured Charlemagne for an excellent pair of clogs. In thanks, the Frankish king gave him a superb cuirass, which he wears to this day.

CASSEL
At crossroads of D916 and D933, 30 km from Dunkerque and 54 km from Calais

It comes as a surprise when the road begins to wind steeply upwards away from the flat fields of Flanders and soars to a delightful little hilltop town, barely more than a village. Most of the way, the road is cobbled – picturesque, perhaps, but also a useful way of making traffic slow down to a civilized pace.

Grand' Place, the long and spacious main square at its centre, attractively paved and cobbled, makes an odd, uneven shape. All around it, the fine Flemish town houses, tall and dignified, have steep roofs and tiers of dormer windows. Several are hotels, cafés and restaurants. Hôtel de la Noble Cour, not a hotel but a grand sixteenth-century mansion, stands out as the very best of them, its stone façade gorgeously carved – and stone was once the very symbol of wealth in this region, where building stone is not locally available. Originally, this was the local lord's court of justice. Inside the house now you'll find a museum with interesting displays about that strange Flemish custom, the *fête géant*. Cassel's own *géant* couple – Reuze-Papa and Reuze-Mama – emerge from the town hall to lead a great procession around the town on Easter Monday. Behind one end of the square, Notre Dame church, an excellent example of Flemish Gothic, completes the picture.

Steep, cobbled paths climb to the summit of the hill (or you can drive to the top), where once there stood a defensive fortress. Today, a pleasant public garden of lawns, flower beds and trees, covers the site, where locals and visitors stroll, play *boules*, or watch the workings of a remarkable eighteenth-century windmill.

Still very much in working order, the windmill can be cranked by hand or, with cloth covers unfurled on to their wooden frames, the sails will turn in the slightest breeze. The whole building, in wood, pivots to meet the wind from whichever direction it comes. It is used even now, though merely as a curiosity, to grind flour.

Also on the hill of Cassel, a tatty, brick building broadcasts Radio Uylenspiegel, the Flemish-language station. In front of it, a monument recalls the Castel of the Romans which stood here two millenia ago, and the several battles which have raged around this spot since then. None were bloodier than during the Great War, whose ghastly progress General Foch oversaw from this hilltop from October 1914 to July 1915. An equestrian statue of him beside the windmill gazes over the field of battle.

Though the altitude is only 176 metres, this hilltop enjoys a thrilling, panoramic view. The old saying may overstate the case, claiming

Hôtel de la Noble Cour, the finest of Cassel's Renaissance mansions, now houses the town's museum

that from Cassel the vista extends into five kingdoms –
Belgium, Holland, France, England and the Kingdom of
God. Before you lies a limitless patchwork across which a
thousand tiny clusters of cottages and clumps of trees have
been scattered. Roads like silver threads pull straight
towards the horizon, water towers point down into the
batteweary earth, while a score of high Flemish steeples
and belfries point to the immense blue dome of the sky.

Museum open April–Oct. a.m. and p.m. Windmill open June–Oct. and school
holidays a.m. and p.m.

AIRE-SUR-LA-LYS
On N43, 50 km from Calais

No longer a village, but a small country town with a pleasant,
welcoming air, Aire is a busy local centre of agriculture and
small industry. On the face of it unpromising – it's on the N43,
has modern outskirts and there's an army base here – the
town reveals its charm only to those who venture away

*Grand' Place in
Aire-sur-la-Lys*

from the main road and into the centre, where the River Lys,
and two canals meet in a confusing tangle of waterways.

The heart of Aire is a huge main square in the shape of a triangle, all constructed between 1720 and 1840. Along one side of this Grand' Place, the fantastically ornate *hôtel de ville* in pale stone has flags hanging from a ceremonial balcony and flowers at the windows. A tall belfry rises from the rear of the building.

On the other two sides of the square, high narrow town houses with steep roofs and dormer windows continue the characteristic Flemish look. Shopfronts, cafés and bars seem rather small around the perimeter of the great *place*. The whole square is cobbled, and although cars may park here, there are usually very few actually parked – giving a sense of immense space and openness.

Main street Rue d'Arras meets Grand' Place at its southern corner, making another little triangular *place* beside the *hôtel de ville*. At the angle, facing the town hall, Le Bailliage is a delightful civic building of brick and stone standing above an arcaded gallery, in elaborate late Renaissance style. Despite the succession of wars which have torn down so much of the region's history, Le Bailliage dates from the 1600s.

Almost as old is the church behind Grand' Place, Église St Jacques, a seventeenth-century Jesuit chapel with an abundance of sculpted decoration. The more impressive St Pierre Collegiate Church, stands on the other side of the Lys in Place St Pierre. Rebuilt at the end of the fifteenth century, when Flanders was at the height of its riches, then carefully restored in 1944 following war damage, it remains one of the most interesting examples of Gothic architecture in Flanders: spacious, inspiring, mainly in lavish flamboyant style, with a mighty and imposing tower over 55 metres tall.

There's a tourist office in the *hôtel de ville*, and a good, popular hotel-restaurant, Les Trois Mousquetaires, which is restful and quiet despite being on the N43.

FROM WESTERN FLANDERS TO EASTERN FLANDERS

While interesting and attractive villages can certainly be found across the whole of the Nord département (or French Flanders), the core of the region, centred on the vast conurbation of Lille-Roubaix, is justly better known for a landscape of highways and railways, manufacturing and mining. The convenient way to by-pass this, and discover the pleasant country of eastern Flanders, is to take *autoroute* A26 from Aire-sur-la-Lys (exits 4 and 5) to Cambrai (exit 8). From Cambrai either travel directly to Le Quesnoy on D942, or take the fast, straight N43 via Le Cateau-Cambrésis.

Henri Matisse Museum (Le Cateau-Cambrésis) open daily a.m. and p.m. excluding Mon., Tue. and fêtes

LE QUESNOY
On D934 and D942, 33 km northeast of Cambrai and 173 km from Calais

Nowadays, the border between France and Belgium is barely noticeable, the roads passing unhindered across the frontier without even the inconvenience of a raised barrier. However, for long centuries the open, vulnerable landscape at France's northern frontier posed serious problems of defense. The area had been contested between the French, the Burgundian dukes, the Hapsburgs, the Holy Roman Empire and the Austrians. A string of heavily fortified towns and villages grew up along the border to guard and protect it from those who would expand their territories, or prevent them from being reduced.

The village of Le Quesnoy has played a fortress role at least since ramparts were built around it in the sixteenth century by Emperor Charles V. A hundred years later the ubiquitous military architect Vauban built a string of forts across Flanders. At Le Quesnoy he recreated the old fortifications, making a magnificent ring of brick ramparts, the main gateways to which had to be reached across wide water defenses. His walls and lakes survive almost intact.

Arriving at the little town you pass through a narrow gate and travel along a cobbled bridge over a dry moat, then across another moat full of water, and across more water – Lac Vauban – with a wall of brick behind. At last, a narrow, heavily fortified gateway is reached, Porte Fauroeulx, and passing through it the road enters the streets of the town.

Just within the gateway, a tourist office can be found on the left, while on the right stone steps lead to the top of the

Bastion Imperial, the inner fortifications, now banked with earth and covered with grass. A footpath, shaded by trees, runs along the top. Fine, sturdy bastions mark the progress of the walls around the town. They have withstood several fierce battles. The most famous seige was one of the most recent: in 1918 the Germans set up camp at Le Quesnoy, confident in the strength of the medieval stronghold. But

Across the moat and through the gateway to enter Le Quesnoy

using an unexpected medieval tactic – climbing the wall with ladders – New Zealand troops gained access to the town and drove out the Germans. There's a monument to their bravery and ingenuity beside the southwest section of the rampart.

The little town has survived its hard, military history with a pleasing provincial air, bustling and cheerful. From Porte Fauroeulx the main street rises to a square with a town hall and church, and descends again to Porte de Valenciennes on the other side.

Along the way are useful shops, cafés, restaurants, all built in the brickwork, often replaced and repaired, so characteristic of Flanders.

LOCQUIGNOL
On D33, 44 km northeast of Cambrai and 195 km from Calais

D33 travels down from Le Quesnoy just 5 kilometres to reach the long, straight D932 from Le Cateau-Cambrésis. Crossing straight over, it continues into the cool, shady woodland of Mormal.

Robert Louis Stevenson, a young man on the first of his foreign adventures, passed by on the other side of the Forêt de Mormal as he paddled along the River Sambre in 1876. He caught only a glimpse of the forest, did not pause, and decided that its name had a sinister ring, as indeed it does.

Yet Mormal provides an oasis of beauty in this strangely featureless landscape. Even in Stevenson's day there was plenty of industry in French Flanders, but in those days Mormal was truly vast. At 8,000 hectares it is still the most extensive woodland in the north, almost all slender beech, and is home to a large deer population. Footpaths and long, straight forest roads, open to the public, run beneath the trees, and meet at junctions with old-fashioned signposts.

In a quiet clearing stands the little village of Locquignol, all of modest, weatherworn brick cottages. Here lived forest labourers and wood craftsmen, from the men who made Flemish clogs to the artists who sculpted wooden church statuary. It remains a hard-working village, with a few fields of cattle at its edges. Their milk goes into the making of Maroilles cheese. On cool evenings the pleasant aroma of woodsmoke rises from the chimneys. A few houses have been made pretty with window boxes, and cobbles revealed along the sides of the highway show how charming the

A pattern in the brickwork echoes the Flemish stepped gable

village could look – if the tarmac were stripped off the pavements.

With its austere brick, and plain architecture, and unpretentious air, the village in the forest nevertheless exerts a curious appeal. In a central square, called simply La Place, a few beech trees shelter some brightly painted café tables, overlooked by the tall spire of a brick church repaired after war damage. At the edge of the village, the cemetery contains the grave of one soldier of the Dorset Regiment, his name 'known only to God'.

PONT-SUR-SAMBRE
On D961, 55 km northeast of Cambrai and 200 km from Calais

Reaching the southeastern side of Mormal forest, an enjoyable country road travels upriver beside the canalized Sambre.

Robert Louis Stevenson's 'gaunt tower with an illegible dialplate'

Stevenson began his *Inland Voyage*, paddling down the Sambre and Oise rivers, at the industrial town of Maubeuge. In those days, too, there was plenty of industry – manufactories whose fires lit up the sky at night. But by the time the river had reached a place called Quartes,

industry had been left behind and a pleasant rurality took over. It's still exactly like that today.

Oddly enough, literary researchers and historians have struggled to discover the whereabouts of Quartes. Perhaps they never came here. Simply by following the Sambre canal you will arrive at 'Lock No 6: Quartes'. This hamlet has become part of the little town of Pont-sur-Sambre, and the 'church on a hill' which Robert Louis Stevenson described as being at Quartes is, indeed, the church of Pont-sur-Sambre.

The river twists right around the town in a great loop, so that from the Quartes lock to the other side of town is 6 kilometres on the water, but only ten minutes on foot. That's why Stevenson (and his friend Sir Walter Grindlay Simpson) abandoned the river at this point and carried their boats through the village of Pont-sur-Sambre. They paused in its main street to look at a 'gaunt tower with an illegible dialplate'.

The old brick tower is still there, on a corner at the end of the simple high street of old and new houses. In fact, it is a clocktower – though with a sundial instead of a clock. The position and the angle of the 'dialplate' make it, if not illegible, then quite incomprehensible. An explanatory plaque at the foot of the tower adds more confusion. Here the little town brushes against the water again. Stevenson and Simpson once more put their boats into the water and paddled away. Beside the river there's a pleasant footpath, with a view of rough pasture and copses on the other side.

MAROILLES
On D962 and D959, 42 km east of Cambrai and 192 km from Calais

No doubt when Stevenson paddled by, 2 kilometres away on the River Sambre, the cheese of Maroilles had little reputation among young Scottish writers. At least, he did not remark on either the village or the cheese for which, in France, it has been acclaimed for centuries. A strongly flavoured cows' milk cheese, Maroilles is thought to have been perhaps the original cheese of the characteristic Flemish type, and certainly was being being made here in the tenth century. Today, Maroilles can be found on the

Made here since the tenth century

cheeseboards of good restaurants all over France, but it still pays to buy the genuine, unpasteurized farm-made product, in its balsawood box, from Maroilles itself. Several shops and houses in the village sell it, and local menus feature tarts and pies with Maroilles cheese.

Despite the one street of the village having become a busy through-road, the village clings to its rustic quality. Across the bottom of the street flows the River Helpe-Mineure. Here a triangular green with cottages arranged on each side lies beside the road which then curves up a hill. Passing a brick and stone church, rising high it reaches another open green with a bandstand in the middle, and brick cottages arranged in a triangle all around. Glance between the houses and only green pasture can be seen behind.

Follow the main road to Avesnes, and from there the country lane D133, wandering from village to village through increasingly attractive farm country.

LIESSIES

On D133, 68 km east of Cambrai and 218 km from Calais

A popular rural base for walkers and cyclists touring this delightful rustic border region, little Liessies consists of a few simple brick and stone houses arranged along a winding village street. There's a *gîte d'étape* (simple hostel), as well as *chambres d'hôtes* (B & Bs), little hotels and inexpensive eating places. At one end, the church, in the fine, blue-tinted grey stone of the region, has its bells hanging outside the black belfry!

Beside the village lies the pleasant, hilly woodland of the Val Joly forest, while 2 kilometres away on D133 the huge, artificial Val Joly lake provides watersports and recreation in the lovely valley of the Helpe-Majeure river. Stay on D133 – which at one point skirts the Belgian border – to follow the valley to Eppe-Sauvage. From there, a quiet lane finds its way to Moustier-en-Fagne.

MOUSTIER-EN-FAGNE

On D83, 70 km east of Cambrai and 220 km from Calais

The lane passes a few isolated cottages, crosses the tiny upper reaches of the River Helpe-Majeure, and finds itself in the tiny hamlet of Moustier-en-Fagne. In old-fashioned, local parlance, *moustier* meant priory, and *fagne* a drained marshy area – of which there were once plenty in this district.

Sure enough, the village consists of little more than a small Benedictine priory, with just a scattering of farmhouses round about. On the left stands a brick and stone manor house, a priory residence. Its gables rise up in steps, and above the lintel and doorposts, made of fine local grey stone with a blue tint, is set a carved stone depicting two angels bearing a crown. High on the wall a pattern of bricks gives the date of the building: 1560.

Across a patch of green, a curious little church, its entrance door the only feature in a bare brick wall, adjoins an arched stone gateway. Through here can be seen the garden of a large mansion which is the abbey. A high wall follows the grounds around, backing on to river and water meadows.

The narrow lane, D83, continues into rough, rolling, green pasture hills. The country becomes all tiny fields, black and white dairy cattle in nearly every one, with plenty of trees and mature hedges. You would hardly recognize it as Flanders; and, indeed, this is the edge of the Belgian Ardennes hills.

The stone doorway of the manor house

WALLERS-TRÉLON
On D83, 70 km east of Cambrai and 220 km from Calais

For shopping, the residents of little Wallers-Trélon nip across the Belgian frontier, barely more than 2 kilometres distant and completely unmarked at this point. This peaceful farming village could easily have been in Belgium, since the border has a rather arbitrary quality, having often slipped a few kilometres either way during the centuries. Between the village and the frontier, a small quarry produces the distinctive local stone, a handsome grey with a hint of blue, known locally simply as *pierre bleue*.

Wallers-Trélon is built almost entirely of this attractive material, austere but pleasing. The solid, substantial stone cottages, under steep roofs of dark grey slate, are set back

A village of fine pierre bleue

from the roadway behind a wide grass verge. A *mairie-école*, a war memorial and a parish church border a small village green. The simple church, in the same grey stone, stands within walled grounds that, with just a dozen graves, can hardly be called a cemetery. Rather, it resembles a lawn. Close to the church, a group of small labourers' cottages in neat terraces front on to their own patch of green, with carefully stacked piles of firewood outside each door. In the village street, in a grand house called the Maison de la Fagne, the Eco-Musée de la Région Fourmies-Trélon tells the story of the local stone and the people who have quarried it, as well as having displays on local architecture, flora and fauna.

The Eco-Musée de la Région Fourmies-Trélon open April–Nov. weekends and fêtes, p.m. only; July–Sept. daily, p.m. only

TOURIST INFORMATION OFFICES

All cities and large towns in France have at least one tourist information office. These have a variety of names, such as Maison du Tourisme or Syndicat d'Initiative. For short, they are all officially known as OTSIs (*Office du Tourisme-Syndicat d'Initiative*). Smaller towns and villages often have an office open only in the peak holiday season (usually July and August) or for a few hours each week. Even where there is no office at all, information for visitors is always available on request at the local *mairie* or *hotel de ville* (town hall).

The following are the main town and city tourist information offices and a selection of village offices in northern France.

PICARDY (WESTERN AND EASTERN)
Aisne, Oise, Pas de Calais, Somme départements

Abbeville
OTSI, Place de l'Amiral Courbet
(tel.: 22 24 27 92)
Open daily all year excluding Mon. a.m.

Aire-sur-la-Lys
Bailliage
(tel.: 21 39 65 66)
Open p.m. daily March–Oct.

Amiens
OTSI, 19 Rue Jean Catelas
(tel.: 22 91 79 28).
Open Mon.–Sat. all year, Sun. in season

Arras
Hôtel de Ville, Place des Héros
(tel.: 21 51 26 95)
Open Mon.–Sat. all year

Beauvais
OTSI, 1 Rue Beauregard
(tel.: 44 45 08 18)
Open daily April–Sept., rest of year Tue.–Sat.

Berck-sur-Mer
OTSI, Place de l'Entonnoir
(tel.: 21 09 50 00)
Open daily in season; closed out of season Sun.

Blérancourt
Mairie
(tel.: 23 39 60 08)
Open all year

Boue
Mairie
(tel.: 23 60 00 68)
Open in season

Boulogne
OTSI, Quai de la Poste
(tel.: 21 31 68 38)
Open daily all year

Calais
OTSI, 12 Boulevard Clemenceau
(tel.: 21 96 62 40)
Open daily all year

Chantilly
OTSI, 23 Avenue du Maréchal Joffre
(tel.: 44 57 08 58)
Open daily (excluding Tue.) all year; May–Sept. only Sun. a.m.

Château Thierry
OTSI, Place de l'Hôtel de Ville
(tel.: 23 83 10 14)
Open daily all year excluding Sun. and fêtes

Compiègne
OTSI, Place de l'Hôtel de Ville
(tel.: 44 40 01 00)
Open daily all year excluding Sun. during 1 Nov.– 15 March

Crécy-en-Ponthieu
Mairie
(tel.: 22 23 54 43)
Open daily all year excluding Mon. and Sat. a.m.

Creil
OTSI, Place du Général de Gaulle
(tel.: 44 55 16 07)
Open daily all year excluding Sun.

Le Crotoy
OTSI, 1 Rue Carnot
(tel.: 22 27 05 25)
Open all year

Doullens
OTSI, Beffroi, Rue du Bourg
(no phone listed)
Open daily 20 June– 1 Nov.

The Villages of Northern France

Ermenonville
OTSI, Parc J. J. Rousseau
(tel.: 44 54 01 58)
Open all year

Etaples
Clos St-Victor, Boulevard
Bigot-Descelers
(tel.: 21 09 56 94)

Fère-en-Tardenois
OTSI, 18 Rue Etienne
Moreau Nelaton
(tel.: 23 82 31 57)
Open 15 April–15 Sept.,
Tue.–Sat., p.m. only;
rest of year Wed. a.m.
and Sat. p.m.

La Ferté Milon
OTSI
(tel.: 23 96 70 45)
Open April–Oct.

Fort-Mahon
OTSI, 1000 Avenue de la
Plage
(tel.: 22 23 36 00)
Open all year

Gerberoy
Mairie
(tel.: 44 82 33 63)

Guise
OTSI
(tel.: 23 60 45 71)
Open daily all year

Hesdin
Mairie
(tel.: 21 86 84 76)

Hirson
3 Rue de Guise
(tel.: 23 58 03 91)
Open all day Mon.
and Sat.; Tue.–Fri.,
p.m. only

Laon
OTSI, Place du Parvis de
la Cathédrale
(tel.: 23 20 28 62)
Open daily all year

Long
OTSI
(tel.: 22 31 82 50)
Open all year

Montreuil-sur-Mer
OTSI, Place Darnétal
(tel.: 21 06 04 27)
Open in season

Noyon
OTSI, Place de l'Hôtel
de Ville
(tel.: 44 44 21 88)
Open daily all year
excluding Sun. and
Mon. a.m.

Pierrefonds
OTSI, Place de l'Hôtel
de Ville
(tel.: 44 42 81 44)
Open daily all year

Rue
OTSI, Mairie
(tel.: 22 25 00 43)
Open all year

St-Omer
OTSI, Boulevard Pierre
Guillain
(tel.: 21 98 08 51)
Open Sat. and Sun.,
May–Sept.

St-Quentin
OTSI, Espace St
Jacques,
Rue de la Sellerie
(tel.: 23 67 05 00)
Open daily all year

St-Riquier
OTSI, Beffroi
(tel.: 22 28 9l 72)
Open occasionally all
year

St-Valery
OTSI, 2 Place Guillaume
le Conquérant
(tel.: 22 60 93 50)
Open daily April–Oct.

Samer
Mairie
(tel.: 21 33 50 64)

Senlis
OTSI, Place du Parvis
Notre-Dame
(tel.: 44 53 06 40)
Open daily excluding
Tue. 1 Feb.–15 Dec.

Septmonts
Mairie
(tel.: 23 74 91 36)
Open all year

Soissons
OTSI, 1 Avenue du
Général Leclerc
(tel.: 23 53 08 27)
Open daily all year
excluding Sun.

Le Touquet
OTSI, Palais de l'Europe
(tel.: 21 85 15 62)
Open all year

Wissant
OTSI, Place de la Mairie
(tel.: 21 85 15 62)
Open all year

NORMANDY

*Upper Normandy only: Eure,
Seine-Maritime with parts of
Calvados and Orne départements*

Les Andelys
OTSI
(tel.: 32 54 41 93)

Bayeux
OTSI, 1 Rue des Cuisiniers
(tel.: 31 92 16 26)
Open daily all year

Caen
OTSI, Hôtel d'Escoville,
Place St Pierre
(tel.: 31 86 27 65)
Open daily all year

Caudebec-en-Caux
OTSI
(tel.: 35 96 20 65)
Open in season

Conches-sur-Ouche
OTSI, Place A. Briand
(tel.: 32 30 91 82)

Deauville
OTSI, Place de la Mairie
(tel.: 31 88 21 43)
Open daily all year
excluding Sun. out of
season

Dieppe
OTSI, Boulevard Général
de Gaulle
(tel.: 35 84 11 77)
Open daily all year

Etretat
OTSI, Place Maurice
Guillard
(tel.: 35 27 05 21)
Open daily March–Oct.

Evreux
OTSI, 1 Place du Général
de Gaulle
(tel.: 32 24 04 43)
Open Mon.–Sat. all year

Fécamp
OTSI, Place Bellet
(tel.: 35 28 20 51)
Open daily all year
excluding Mon.

Gerberoy
(Oise département) see
under Picardy

Giverny
Monet's house and garden
(tel.: 32 51 28 21)

Le Havre
Forum de l'Hôtel de Ville
(tel.: 35 21 22 88)
Open daily all year

Honfleur
OTSI, Place Boudin
(tel.: 31 89 23 30)

Open daily all year
excluding Sun. out of
season

Lisieux
OTSI, 11 Rue d'Alençon
(tel.: 31 62 08 41)
Open daily all year
excluding Sun. out of
season

Livarot
OTSI, 1 Place Georges
Bisson
(tel.: 31 63 47 39)
Open daily April–Sept.,
out of season weekends
only

Lyons-la-Forêt
OTSI
(tel.: 32 49 31 65)

Orbec
OTSI, Rue Guillonière
(tel.: 31 32 87 15)

Pont l'Evêque
Hôtel de Brilly
(tel.: 31 64 12 77)
Open daily all year

Rouen
OTSI, 25 Place de la
Cathédrale
(tel.: 35 71 41 77)
Open daily all year
excluding Sun. out of
season

St-Valery-en-Caux
OTSI, Place de l'Hôtel
de Ville
(tel.: 35 97 00 63)
Open daily May–Sept.,
a.m. out of season
Wed.–Sun.

Le Tréport
OTSI
(tel.: 35 86 05 67)

Vernon
OTSI, 36 Rue Carnot
(tel.: 32 51 39 60)

Vimoutiers
OTSI, 10 Avenue Général
de Gaulle
(tel.: 33 39 30 29)
Open daily all year
excluding Sat. p.m.,
Sun., Mon. a.m.

Yvetot
OTSI, Place Victor Hugo
(tel.: 35 95 08 40)
Open 15 June–30 Sept.

CHAMPAGNE, LORRAINE, ARDENNES
*Ardennes, Aube, Haute-Marne,
Marne, Meurthe-et-Moselle,
Meuse, Moselle, Vosges
départements*

Ambonnay
Mairie
(tel.: 26 57 01 07)

Aÿ
7 Avenue de Champagne
(tel.: 26 55 33 00)

Bains-les-Bains
OTSI, Place du Bain
Romain
(tel.: 29 36 31 75)
Open daily in season

Bar-le-Duc
12 Rue Lapique
(tel.: 29 79 11 13)
Open in season

Bouzy
Mairie, Place de l'Église
(tel.: 26 57 00 32)

Châlons-sur-Marne
OTSI, 3 Quai des Arts
(tel.: 26 65 17 89)
Open daily all year
excluding Sun.

Charleville-Mezières
OTSI, 4 Place Ducade
(tel.: 24 33 00 17)
Open daily all year

The Villages of Northern France

Châtillon-sur-Marne
At statue of Urban II
and 11 Rue de l'Église
(tel.: 26 58 34 66)
Open in season

Clermont-en-Argonne
13 Place de la République
(no phone number given)

Contrexeville
OTSI, Galerie du Parc
(tel.: 29 08 08 68)
Open daily April–Oct.,
Mon.–Fri. out of season

Dormans-en-Champagne
OTSI, Rue du Pont
(tel.: 26 58 21 45)
Open May–Oct. p.m.
only Tues.–Sat.

Epernay
OTSI, 7 Avenue de
Champagne
(tel.: 26 55 33 00)
Open daily all year
excluding Sun. out of
season

Epinal
OTSI, 13 Rue de la
Comédie
(tel.: 29 82 53 32)
Open Mon.–Sat. all year,
Sun. in season

Gérardmer
OTSI, Place des Deportés
(tel.: 29 63 08 74)
Open daily all year
excluding Sun. out of
season

Lac du Der Chantecoq
Maison du Lac,
Giffaumont-Champaubert
(tel.: 26 72 62 80)

Lunéville
OTSI, Aile Sud du
Château
(tel.: 83 74 06 55)
Open daily all year

Metz
OTSI, Place d'Armes
(tel.: 87 75 65 21)
Open daily in season,
Mon.–Fri. out of season

Montmédy-Haut
Beside main gate
(tel.: 29 80 15 90)
Open daily Feb.–Nov.

Mouzon
Mairie
(tel.: 24 26 10 63)

Nancy
OTSI, 14 Place Stanislas
(tel.: 83 35 22 41)
Open daily all year

Plombières-les-Bains
OTSI, 16 Rue Stanislas
(tel.: 29 66 01 30)
Open all year

Reims
OTSI, Square du Trésor,
2 Rue Guillaume-
de-Machault
(near cathedral)
(tel.: 26 47 25 69)
Open daily all year

Remiremont
OTSI, 2 Place H. Utard
(tel.: 29 62 23 70)
Open Mon.–Sat.
all year

Rethel
Hôtel de Ville
(tel.: 24 38 52 16)
Open all year

Rocroi
OTSI, Place André
Hardy
(tel.: 24 54 11 75)
Open all year

St-Dizier
OTSI, Pavillon du Jard
(tel.: 25 05 31 84)
Open daily all year
excluding Sun.

Ste-Menehould
OTSI, Place Leclerc
(tel.: 26 60 85 83)

Sezanne
OTSI, Place de la
République
(tel.: 26 80 51 43)
Open daily all year
excluding Sun. and
Mon.

Stenay
Hôtel de Ville
(tel.: 29 80 30 31)
Open daily in season

Thionville
OTSI, 16 Rue du Vieux-
Collège
(tel.: 82 53 33 18)
Open Mon.–Sat. all year

Toul
OTSI, Place du Parvis de
la Cathédrale
(tel.: 83 64 11 69)
Open daily all year
excluding Sun. and fêtes

Troyes
OTSI, 16 Boulevard
Carnot
(tel.: 25 73 00 36)
Open daily all year

Varennes-en-Argonne
Hôtel de Ville
(tel.: 29 80 71 01)
Open in season

Verdun
OTSI, Place de la Nation
(tel.: 29 86 14 18)
Open daily all year

Verzy
Mairie
(tel.: 26 97 90 91)
Open Mon.–Fri.

Vittel
OTSI, Avenue Bouloumie
(tel.: 29 08 37 37)
Open all year

ALSACE
*Bas-Rhin, Haute-Rhin
départements*

Andlau
Place de l'Hôtel de Ville
(tel.: 88 08 22 57)
Open July–Sept.

Barr
Place de l'Hôtel de Ville
(tel.: 88 08 94 24)
Open all year

Colmar
OTSI, 4 Rue des
Unterlinden
(tel.: 89 41 02 29)
Open daily all year

Dambach-la-Ville
Mairie
(tel.: 88 92 61 00)
Open all year

Haut-Koenigsbourg
Nearest tourist office in
Kintzheim

Le Hohwald
OTSI
(tel.: 88 08 33 92)
Open all year

Kaysersberg
Hôtel de Ville
(tel.: 89 78 22 78)
Open daily all year

Kintzheim
Place de la Fontaine
(tel.: 88 82 09 90)
Open daily June–
Sept.

Molsheim
Mairie
(tel.: 88 38 52 00)
Open all year

Mulhouse
OTSI, 9 Avenue Maréchal
Foch
(tel.: 89 45 68 31)
Open daily all year

excluding Sun. out of
season

Niederbronn-les-Bains
OTSI, 2 Place de l'Hôtel
de Ville
(tel.: 88 09 17 00)
Open Mon.–Fri. all
year

Obernai
Chapelle du Beffroi
(tel.: 88 95 64 13)
Open daily in season,
Mon.–Fri. out of season

Otrott
Mairie
(tel.: 88 95 64 13)
Open July–Sept.

Saverne
Chapelle des Rohans,
Place du Général de
Gaulle
(tel.: 88 91 80 47)

Sélestat
OTSI, Commanderie St
Jean, Boulevard Leclerc
(tel.: 88 92 02 66)
Open daily all year

Strasbourg
OTSI offices at
Place de la Gare
(tel.: 88 32 51 49),
Place Gutenberg
(tel.: 88 32 57 07),
Pont de l'Europe
(tel.: 88 61 39 23).
All open daily all year

Turckheim
OTSI, Place Turenne
(tel.: 89 27 38 44)
Open daily all year

Wasselonne
OTSI, Place Général
Leclerc
(tel.: 88 87 17 22)
Open daily 15 June–
15 Sept.

FLANDERS
Nord département

Aire-sur-la-Lys
(Pas de Calais) see
under Picardy

Arras
(Pas de Calais) see
under Picardy

Avesnes
OTSI, Maison du
Chanoine,
Place Maréchal Leclerc
(tel.: 27 57 92 40)
Open Mon.–Sat. all year,
Sun. in season

Bergues
OTSI, Beffroi
(tel.: 28 68 60 44)
Open daily in season
excluding Fri.; Sun. out
of season

Bray Dunes
OTSI, Place J. Rubben
(tel.: 28 26 64 25)
Open daily all year
excluding Sun. p.m.

Cambrai
OTSI, 48 Rue de Noyon
(tel.: 27 78 26 90)

Cassel
OTSI, Grand' Place
(tel.: 28 40 52 55)
Open daily in season

Le Cateau Cambrésis
OTSI, Place Fénelon
(tel.: 27 84 10 94)
Open Wed.–Sun. all year

Douai
Hôtel du Dauphin,
70 Place d'Armes
(tel.: 27 88 26 79)
Open Mon.–Sat. a.m.
all year

Dunkerque
Beffroi

The Villages of Northern France

(tel.: 28 66 79 21)
Open daily all year
excluding Sun.
Esquelbecq
Mairie, Place A.
Bergerot
(tel.: 28 65 63 16)
Gravelines
OTSI, 11 Rue de la
République
(tel.: 28 23 39 16)
Open daily all year
Hondschoote
Mairie
(tel.: 28 68 31 55)
Open all year
Lille
Palais Rihour, Place
Rihour
(tel.: 20 30 81 00)
Open daily all year

Maroilles
OTSI, Grand' Rue
(tel.: 27 84 72 33)
Open June–Sept. Sun.
a.m. only
Maubeuge
OTSI, Porte de Bavay,
Avenue du Parc
(tel.: 27 62 11 93)
Open daily all year
Le Quesnoy
1 Rue Maréchal Joffre
(tel.: 27 49 05 28)
Open Mon.–Sat. a.m. all
year; Sat. p.m. and Sun.
in season
Roubaix
Hôtel de Ville, 17 Grand'
Place
(tel.: 20 73 70 19)
Open daily all year

St-Omer
(Pas de Calais) see
under Picardy
Steenvoorde
Hôtel de Ville
(tel.: 28 43 32 60)
Tourcoing
OTSI, Parvis St
Christophe
(tel.: 20 26 89 03)
Open daily all year
Trélon
Mairie
(tel.: 27 59 75 00)
Open Easter–Sept.
Valenciennes
OTSI, Maison Espagnole,
1 Rue Askièva
(tel.: 27 46 22 99)
Open p.m. daily all year
excluding Sun.

INDEX OF PLACES

The Villages of Northern France